*Twayne's United States Authors Series*

Sylvia E. Bowman, *Editor*

INDIANA UNIVERSITY

*Roger Williams*

*Statue of Roger Williams overlooking downtown Providence, Rhode Island*

# ROGER WILLIAMS

# ROGER WILLIAMS

## by HENRY CHUPACK

Kingsborough Community College
of the City University of New York

 157

Twayne Publishers, Inc.    ::    New York

To Leah With Love

# ROGER WILLIAMS

## by

## HENRY CHUPACK

Perhaps not since colonial times has the issue of separation of church and state been more in the news and its basic premises more hotly debated and questioned than in the generation since the end of World War II. Thus, this new study of *Roger Williams* should prove invaluable in determining whether the principles he enunciated are still viable for Americans of the Space Age. And if his ideas concerning the relationship between church and state are an established way of thinking on the part of a good many Americans today, the reader is not allowed to forget that Williams was in fact the first important figure in American life who was anti-establishment. Here the ruling group was the Massachusetts Bay oligarchy who regarded his emphasis on the need to keep the spiritual and civil spheres clear and distinct from one another as pure heresy and consequently banished him from their midst.

Anti-establishment as he was, Williams was still far from being the great political democrat which many of his biographers have pictured him in light of his having founded Providence as a haven for the religiously oppressed. Instead, this study will furnish evidence that Williams conceived political liberty as not an end in itself, but merely as a means toward establishing a society in which people were free solely to work out their own place in the spiritual scheme of things.

Thus a decidedly new insight is given of Williams as one who was primarily interested in the things of the spirit rather than in politics.

# Preface

Separation of church and state and absolute freedom of conscience, the two major principles for which Roger Williams is best known, and both of which became part of the mainstream of American thought with the adoption of the Bill of Rights, are as fraught with significance for our times as when Williams originally espoused them. In the past few years, two countries in which both principles have more than come under their share of attack or support have been Vietnam and the United States. Newspaper pictures of Buddhist monks cremating themselves to protest the religious restrictions placed upon them by the Vietnamese government do not appear as frequently as they used to; however, there are still many Americans who feel that in outlawing prayers in public schools, the Supreme Court took a giant step toward atheism or worse.

More recently the Johnson administration's $1.3 billion school-aid bill, dispensing large sums to both public and private church-related schools, is even now being contested by many thoughtful Americans as a grave violation of church-state separation. An even more recent expression of the divisiveness which confronts Americans on this score took place at the New York State Constitutional Convention held in the summer of 1967, when one of the major issues which the legislators had to contend with was the increasing pressure by the Catholic hierarchy to repeal the Blaine Amendment, which prohibited direct or indirect aid to parochial education.

Thomas Jefferson, whose views on religious toleration are often compared with those of Williams, believed that every generation had to undergo a revolution in order to remain dynamically alive. In a similar sense, Williams' ideas and the underlying reasoning behind them need to be reexamined from time to time, since the sane lessons they teach have as yet not been completely absorbed by his countrymen, let alone by those in other parts of the world.

Therefore, no apology need be made for still another study of the controversial thinker about whom more has been written than any other colonial figure. Yet through the years so effusive have been the depictions of the Rhode Islander as a political and religious liberal, that it took the late Perry Miller's exhaustive work on the New England mind to remind us that Williams lived under a Calvinistic order of ideas like predestination and the total depravity of man, in a mental and theological frame of reference completely opposed to the intellectual milieus which nineteenth- and twentieth-century biographers tried to invest him with. But with the publication in 1952 of an article entitled "Neglected Aspects of Roger Williams' Thought" (*Church History*, XXI, 239–58) by Mauro Calamandrei, it became apparent that Williams' theological orientation played a far more important part in the molding of his political and social ideas than had been previously acknowledged.

After the appearance of "The Theology and Political Thought of Roger Williams" in 1953, the doctoral thesis from which the aforementioned article was an excerpt, it was necessary for all studies to start with Mr. Calamandrei's essay if a true picture of Williams was to emerge from the welter of misconceptions and distortions to which he had been subjected from well-meaning but insufficiently informed historians and biographers. But before a start at this new evaluation can be made, any real understanding of Williams' thinking is dependent upon a knowledge of seventeenth-century England and what was to become that age's most powerful religious and political movement, the thrust of Puritanism. The Puritans, as the followers of this movement came to be called in Elizabeth's reign, became involved in politics only when they found their efforts at purifying the Church of England almost totally blocked by Elizabeth and then later by the Stuarts. To be sure, by 1660, when "normalcy," so to speak, returned to England with the restoration of Charles II, the set of ideas constituting the Puritan complex had largely spent itself. But by that time Puritanism had completely revolutionized English life and thought and had also left its imprint permanently on American life.

For the dynamism which animated the Puritans in the first five decades of the seventeenth century was to produce, among other things, the following results at home and abroad: the energy and zeal responsible for the colonization of New England; the determination not to yield to the divine-right theory with which the Stuarts opposed the Puritans, a position culminating in the Puritan Revolution and decisively modifying for all time the nature of English sovereignty in favor of Parliament; and finally, the form for the expression of the fierce religious disputes of the age from which the idea of toleration permanently emerged and gradually permeated the *modus operandi* of both English and American religious life.

The forces behind these events are not easy to define, especially when the Puritans set out originally only to reform a church they thought had been corrupted by its previous association with Rome. Our purpose will be served, however, if the basis of Puritanism is seen as residing in a firm religious conviction that its adherents, thanks to God's providence, had been elected to live eternally, while the rest of mankind was consigned to damnation. Initiated in good measure by Luther's conviction that only by a right personal relationship with Deity could man gain salvation, and later codified by Calvin into a five-point theological system, Puritanism was characterized at the outset by the act of conversion on the part of its adherents; and those undergoing this experience felt they had literally seen God face to face and thus were saved. This state of mind, akin to Augustine's concept of the restless soul having found rest in God, made these newly transformed souls think of themselves as latter-day saints whose sole objective was to bring the rule of God to earth.

Following their conversion, many may have had doubts about their election; but, by and large, most Puritans never lost their assurance that they alone were the elect and had only to persevere strenuously in righteousness to earn their eternal reward. To help them remain steadfast there was the Bible, the one book they all studied very carefully to better determine God's will for his saints. When viewed in this light, the Puritans can be seen as an aggregation of tremendously forceful people who brooked no interference with what they considered to be the will of God. Such earnest religionists, dedicated to the idea that the saints were to rule as God's vicegerents on earth, would in the course of time sweep away ideas and men of lesser strength and conviction, as Charles I and the Royalists learned to their dismay.

Puritanism was of course many other things, but the point is that in the seventeenth century it included among its many adherents men and women from the various stratas of English life who believed that—very much like the Hebrews of the Old Testament—in an idolatrous age God's grace had been accorded them. Their function henceforth would be to lead the rest of sinful mankind out of the darkness into which the Antichrist had plunged it.

It was in fact how far the Puritans in Massachusetts Bay were prepared to go to save mankind that caused the split between them and Williams. It will be the thesis of this book to prove that for Williams, the religious policies pursued by the theocracy in the Bay Colony as well as by the Congregationalists and Presbyterians in England, were simply not holy or righteous enough to lead the mass of unregenerate mankind out of its thralldom. His own conviction that people should be left free to make their own choices in matters of faith clashed head-on with those who were intent upon forcing the unregenerate into prescribed forms of worship, a coercion hastened materially by the civil magistrate. Yet if Rhode Island under the aegis of Williams became a colony where freedom from compulsion in religious matters obtained, this freedom of itself meant little to him. For him, men were at civil liberty not to remain unregenerate but to choose their respective faiths without molestation from the civil authorities. And even when people had chosen their respective faiths free from coercion, he was not the religious liberal he has been pictured, as the Quakers who settled in Rhode Island were to find out. In this disparate light, then, of both rebel and conservative are Williams' controversial tracts to be understood and properly assessed.

No attempt, however, will be made to enter the many areas of controversy to which Williams' dynamic ideas naturally lent themselves; a far larger book would be neeeded for that intention. Instead, this study will examine Williams' theology in order to explain the fundamental basis of his thinking. And besides the presentation of the ascertained biographical facts and the major ideas in his tracts, a cursory review of recent research and an estimate of his relevance for our day will also be given. Accordingly, Chapter 1 will deal with the details of Williams' life in England and sketch the historical, political, and religious background from which he emerged, together with an account of the more important influences that molded his thought and character. Chapter 2 will be given over to the important events of his New England years: his disputes with the Massachusetts Bay oligarchy and his consequent banishment; the founding of Providence and the subsequent colonization of Rhode Island; and his later years as a kind of seventeenth-century Bernard Baruch, an elder statesman giving unselfishly of himself and his time whenever Rhode Island needed his services.

An examination of his tracts published abroad constitutes Chapters 3 and 4, with the former devoted to the following works printed during his first sojourn in England: *A key into the Language of America, Mr. Cotton's Letter Examined and Answered, Queries of Highest Consideration, The Bloudy Tenent of Persecution,* and *Christenings Make Not Christians.* Chapter 4 delves into the works published during his second stay in the mother country: *Experiments of Spiritual Life and Health, Major Butler's Fourth Paper, The Bloody Tenent Yet More Bloody, The Hireling Ministry,* and *The Examiner.*

Chapter 5 is concerned with an investigation of the only work Williams managed to have published in New England, *George Fox Digg'd Out of His Burrowes,* while the concluding chapter attempts an assessment of Williams' thinking and its significance for our times.

For the many historians and biographers whose works have prepared the way for this study, I am exceedingly grateful. Still special thanks must be given to two unpublished doctoral dissertations: Mr. Calamandrei's and Clarence S. Roddy's "The Religious Thought of Roger Williams," written in 1948. Note: I have quoted extensively from Williams' tracts in order to give some sense of the mental and spiritual flavor of the man as well as to buttress points I wish to make. Accordingly, in Chapters 3–5 I have indicated each of the tracts by a separate footnote; quotations that follow with their page numbers inserted parenthetically in the text will be understood to allude to the particular work for which the footnote was given.

HENRY CHUPACK

*Kingsborough Community College
of the City University of
New York*

# Contents

Contents

# Chronology

1603 Accession of James I; probable date of Roger Williams' birth.

1617 Employment as stenographer to Sir Edward Coke.

1620 Pilgrims land at Plymouth.

1621 Williams student at Charterhouse.

1623– Williams a Charterhouse scholar at Pembroke Hall, Cam-
1629 bridge.

1625 Accession of Charles I.

1629 Williams chaplain in household of Sir William Masham at Otes, Essex; marries Mary Barnard.

1630 The "Great Migration" to Massachusetts Bay; December 1: Williams and wife leave England.

1631 Williams arrives at Boston (February 5); refuses offer of Boston pulpit; harried out of a position in Salem; leaves for Plymouth.

1633 Williams minister in Salem.

1635 Dispute with Massachusetts Bay officials; October 9: Williams sentenced to banishment.

1636 January: Williams flees from Salem; summer: settlement of Providence.

1636– Pequot War.
1637

1637– Antinomian heresy in Massachusetts; Anne Hutchinson and
1638 Antinomians leave for Rhode Island.

1639 Williams becomes a "Seeker" after a short period as a Baptist.

1642 English Civil Wars begin.

1643 Williams in London to obtain charter for Rhode Island.

1644 March 14: Charter granted to Rhode Island; July 15: publication of The Bloudy Tenent.

1649 January 30: execution of Charles I.

1651–  Williams second sojourn in London.
1654

1652  Publication of *The Bloody Tenent Yet More Bloody*.

1654–  Williams President of Rhode Island.
1657

1660  Restoration of Charles II.

1663  Royal charter granted Rhode Island.

1668–  Disputes between Rhode Island and Connecticut over Nar-
1670  ragansett lands.

1672  Williams' debate with Quakers.

1675–  King Philip's War.
1676

1683  Death of Roger Williams.

*Roger Williams*

CHAPTER *1*

# The Background of a Separatist

THERE can be no valid comprehension of Roger Williams without the realization that the fundamental cast of his mind was religious, and that his political and social ideas were of lesser importance than some biographers have ascribed to them. One statement from *Experiments of Spiritual Life and Health*, a brief summary of his religious beliefs, is indicative of his habitual view toward existence: "Our very life and being is but a swift and short passage from the bank of time to the other side . . . of a dolefull eternity." [1] Another passage on the same page that counsels patience in the midst of adversities bids us remember that our short span of life is intended to purge and fit us "for an eternall Glory."

Yet in spite of the deeply spiritual bent of the above statements, most people still think of Williams as an early apostle and practitioner of democracy. This liberal version of the man is mainly derived from nineteenth-century historians like George Bancroft and others who wrote from the perspective occasioned by the political and social revolution brought on by Andrew Jackson's administration. Even as late as 1927, this romantic view prevailed when Vernon Parrington viewed Williams as "primarily a political philosopher rather than a theologian." [2] Time has since disproved Parrington's thesis that the best in American thought evolved from Jeffersonian liberalism, in which assessment Williams was included among those of our early writers who foreshadowed this kind of thinking. Nevertheless, Parrington's evaluation of Williams has remained the dominant one; and nearly all of Williams' biographers since the 1920's have portrayed him as a foremost democrat and liberal, and have given scant attention to his religious beliefs. [3]

As we shall see, Williams was a fervent Puritan who was interested in political democracy only as this form of government made possible a civil state and a mental climate more conducive for the elect to better commune with their Maker. And, though he stood for absolute freedom of conscience, he was far from being a liberal, if by that term is meant one who espoused complete freedom of thought. When serving as President of Rhode Island, he was not at all timid in haling into court offenders who, under the guise of religious freedom, were disturbing the civil peace. Williams must be viewed, therefore, against the background of his age, and this will show him to be a courageous and admirable figure, but for reasons other than those commonly entertained of him.

## I  *Historical Setting*

Roger Williams was born into a seventeenth-century England which was still recovering from the severe dislocation brought on by the Reformation of the previous century. Where previously Catholicism had been the official religion, thanks to the ferment caused by the Reformation and Henry VIII's desire to break away from papal jurisdiction, the Act of Supremacy passed by the Parliament in 1534 established the Church of England—or the Anglican Church as it came to be known—with Henry proclaimed as its only supreme head. Since this newly instituted national church retained many of the old Catholic rituals and merely substituted the authority of the state for that of the Roman Church many Englishmen both within and outside its fold were less than enthusiastic with only the façade of change.

Easily the greatest dissenters inside the Church were the Puritans, a left-wing faction of Anglicans who were intent upon a wholesale reformation of the institution and were allowed ample freedom during Elizabeth's reign so long as their religious practices did not impugn her position as the spiritual head of the church. Repulsed by her in their efforts for additional reform of the ecclesiastical establishment, the Puritans remained content to add converts rapidly to their way of thinking. In time they hoped to take over the Anglican Church, which would still remain a state church, although it would be a theocracy rather than an episcopacy, and one more in line with their Calvinistic principles of simplicity of service and semiautonomous organization.

But as would be expected from a religious movement in which

Luther had made it clear that every man was his own priest and prophet, there were even among the Puritans themselves radicals like Robert Browne, who rather than wait to remodel the Anglican Church, wished most of all to be removed from it. For to the Brownists, as the followers of Browne came to be called, the state church was hopelessly corrupt because of its papist derivation, and in the 1580's they simply separated from it to hold their own autonomous services. Hated alike by the Anglicans who felt their church was being vilified, and by the Puritans who regarded their removal from the Church of England as a distinct rebuke to their own position of compromise, the Brownists attracted to their ranks the more radical Puritans who saw in separation the only means of instituting a true church. And despite the compromise which Elizabeth pushed through to hold the various disparate religious groups in hand, the number of Puritans and Nonconformists grew rapidly during her reign, a situation that was to plague her Stuart successors, James I and his son Charles I.

The remarkable growth of the Puritans was in fact to provide the impetus for the second jarring upheaval England was to undergo within the course of a century. For the religious dissension between the Anglican episcopacy and the Puritans, which came to a head during the reign of Charles I, became entwined simultaneously with the struggle for political sovereignty being waged between the Stuarts and their subjects and ended eventually in the Puritan Revolution and the emergence of Cromwell as Lord Protector of the English nation. As a product of his time, Roger Williams was deeply influenced by both the heterodox thinking brought on by the Reformation and the political issues that underlay the conflict between the Stuart court and Parliament. And for the increasingly dark political and religious atmosphere in which Williams grew up, one man alone, King James, was largely responsible, as a glance at his policies reveals.

When James asserted in his *True Law of Free Monarchies* (1598) that kings ruled solely by divine right and were responsible to God alone for their actions, Englishmen must have groaned at the inability of Elizabeth's Scottish successor to read the signs of the changing political times. True, that after his break with Rome, Henry VIII had also voiced the idea of divine right; but he and his daughter Elizabeth had trod gingerly on this issue, and had never openly denied the rights of Parliament. But with

James's accession in 1603, the medieval concept of king in parliament, which had prevailed hitherto, was subjected to severe stress as a result of the Scottish king's absolutist ideas and his efforts to nullify Parliament as a coequal with him in matters of government. Thus began the battle for political supremacy, a contest not to be resolved until the Glorious Revolution of 1688, which saw the will of the people as expressed by Parliament emerge the victor.

But while James was king, middle-class Englishmen who had enjoyed rights and privileges unchallenged since the Magna Charta (1215) were not disposed to give them up or to regard them as simply a grant (as James said they were); nor were they deeply impressed with James's theory of divine right. With their newly won sense of importance because of the wealth they had amassed as a continuing result of the Commercial Revolution, these bourgeoisie, their ranks augmented by the ambitious and educated lesser gentry, were eager for even more rights than those they already enjoyed. But James was hostile to any changes that meant an extension of Parliament's power. Hence his collisions with the three Parliaments he called into session during his reign, especially with the last one in 1623.

For this Parliament in *The Great Protestation* informed the king that "the liberties, franchises, privileges and jurisdiction of Parliament are the ancient and undoubted birthright and inheritance of the subjects of England, and that the arduous and urgent affairs concerning the king, state and defense of the realm . . . are proper subjects and matter of council and debate in Parliament." The tyranny of James and later of Charles in ruling autocratically after the dismissal of their several respective Parliaments would not be lost on the future founder of Rhode Island, whose first step in Providence was to institute a government run and controlled by the settlers.

Political strife, though, was merely one side of the coin in the contest for sovereignty between James and his subjects. The other was the growing religious opposition of the Puritans to the concept of a national church headed by the king. Although their efforts at purifying the church during Elizabeth's reign had failed, the Puritans had hoped with the advent of James to substitute a more simplified form of worship for the more elaborate rites of the Anglicans. These hopes were soon crushed by the results of the Hampton Court Conference of 1604, which demanded strict conformity to the ritual of the Church of England. Because of this and other rebuffs by the Stuarts, which made church reforms seem all but hopeless, Puritans by the thousands emigrated to New England in the 1630's to establish their own church governments in the wilderness. Those who remained in England were ultimately driven to revolt against Charles I; and, despite the hardships they endured, most of them, during the first three decades of the century, still yearned to impose their own brand of church government in the land, a rule which would have substituted a theocracy for the Anglican episcopacy.

On the other hand, the more radical among them, despairing of ever cleaning up the corruptions of the established church by remaining within its confines, became Separatists. It was as a Separatist that Roger Williams encountered difficulty at the hands of the authorities in both old and New England. How and why he became affiliated with this radical faction can be learned by a study of those influences in his early life which molded his religious convictions.

## II   *Early Years in Smithfield*

Williams' year of birth has never been ascertained because the register of St. Sepulchre's, the ancient church of the parish in which he was probably born, was destroyed in the Great London Fire of 1666. What Thomas Dekker termed "the wonderful yeare, 1603" [4] is still the likeliest one. Williams himself is no great help, since the few entries in his works and in early offical documents have his year of birth, with one exception, ranging from 1602 to 1606.[5]

Equally disconcerting is the little knowledge available of the forebears of Roger's father, James Williams, whom history records as having been a "citizen and merchant taylor of London." As a member of this once powerful guild of merchant taylors, James Williams, from all available evidence, managed to support his family in moderate if not luxurious circumstances.[6] Of his influence on his later famous son or the two older children Sydrach and Catherine, as well as on the youngest child Robert, there is nothing on record.

More is known of Roger's mother, Alice Williams, née Pemberton, whose family was one of the lesser landed gentry that came into prominence during the reign of Henry VIII. Born in Saint Albans, Hertfordshire, Alice had two brothers, Roger and James, who gained some local fame. Roger Pemberton after whom his nephew was named, became High Sheriff of his county in 1618, while his brother James served as Lord Mayor of London from 1611 to 1612.[7] Alice Pemberton Williams, who appears to have been better off financially than her husband, had an income from several pieces of property which she owned;[8] but, as in the case of her husband, nothing is known of any influence she may have had on any of her offspring. But, because of her family background, her children no doubt became aware of the amenities which middle-class life afforded.

Roger's formative years were spent in Smithfield, a fantastically busy suburb located just outside the old city walls in the northwestern section of overpopulated London. With its "divers fair inns and other comely buildings"[9] erected as a result of a building boom, by the early 1600's Smithfield had become the center of London's trade, with its well-to-do tradesmen diligently employed in selling their wares. No records exist of Roger's early education, but an elementary school was known to have been located in St. Sepulchre's parish, which he most likely started attending at the age of six. There he would have been taught such educational staples as religion, writing, grammar and have learned to read both Latin and English. Learning was an arduous process in these formative years, with school taking some ten or eleven hours daily. Whether absorbing his "Pettyes and Punies" as the rudiments at elementary school were called, or attending the grammar school, the second step in his education, the major emphasis was on complete mastery of the subject matter, an objective attained by incessant repetition of the material. That the curriculum had very little relation to the life being lived outside of school did not matter. Students were expected to learn what was set before them; and, in most cases, fathers took excessive pride in their sons' mastery of Latin.[10]

Yet for all the time it consumed, formal learning played but one part in the young boy's life. For enjoyment there was the Thames River only a half mile from Cow Lane where his family had its home, and where his father probably used the front part of the house as his shop. On the long wharves of the busy river, the incoming cargoes of tobacco from newly settled Virginia made young Roger early aware of lands across the sea to which some of his countrymen had already migrated. On the wharves, too, he probably absorbed the atmosphere of the sea, which later found expression in the many nautical images he employed in his writings. Again, visits to London in 1612 by Captain John Smith and in 1616 by Pocahontas served only to make more concrete and vivid the facts of English colonization that the boy absorbed during his rambles on the docks. In 1609, only two years after the settlement of Jamestown, the Merchant Taylors, along with other guilds, were asked to contribute their share of the costs for colonial enterprises being contemplated by the city fathers to ease the then existing population explosion. Even at the age of six, considering the maturity required of children who attended school for almost half a day, Roger may have understood in some degree the implications of the financial help being exacted from such men as his father and his fellow workers.[11]

For children and adults alike the entertainment treat of the year in Smithfield was the annual St. Bartholomew Fair. Originally conceived as a religious observance, the holy day had been gradually transformed into a great Cloth Fair where, for several days each August, Londoners had the opportunity to enjoy a riotous and fun-loving atmosphere. Gaiety, however, was but a short-lived matter in a district where martyrs were still going to the stake because of their beliefs. As late as March, 1611, Bartholomew Legate, a lay preacher turned heretic, was put to death, and among the many victims claimed previously by the stake had been the much-loved vicar of St. Sepulchre's, John Rogers, who, in 1555, paid with his life for beliefs distasteful to the then reigning monarch, Queen Mary.

Two references in Roger Williams' writings referring to his early years indicate that from the very beginning religion was the foremost influence in the boy's life. One allusion dealt with his early conversion to Puritanism: "From my Childhood the Father of Lights and Mercies toucht my Soul with a Love to himself, to his only begotten, the true Lord Jesus, to his holy Scriptures."[12] But the Puritan ideas and insights gained from Roger's soul having been "toucht" may not have been entirely compatible with those of his father, an Anglican businessman whose guild from time to time did business with the Stuart court. This is seen in a remark Williams made to John Winthrop in 1632: "Myself a child in everything though in Christ called and persecuted in and out of my father's house these 20 years." [13]

What persecution he may have been subjected to, we do not know. But from his ninth year when he may have begun reading the recently published King James Bible and John Foxe's *Book of Martyrs*, the youngster must have become aware of the enormous risks one undertook in holding to unorthodox beliefs. If the martyrdom of Legate in 1611 was not enough of a reminder, there was the living example of the constant ill will and rough treatment afforded a group of some four hundred and fifty French and Dutch refugees who lived in the Smithfield area.[14] Though granted royal permission to engage in their unorthodox worship, these aliens, who prayed at the church of Austin Friars,[15] were daily subjected to the abuse and vilification of their Anglican neighbors who held their own services at St. Sepulchre's. That these foreigners also competed with the native Englishmen as tradesmen may have been another reason for the hostility borne them.

In 1604, James I had promised the Puritans he would have them conform to Anglican ritual or else harry them out of the land. They reacted by remaining within the framework of the established church; however, the more conservative element among them, the Presbyterians, were all the more determined to overthrow the episcopacy and to substitute their own presbyters as the ruling body of the Anglican Church. A smaller group of Puritans, who had recently become Nonseparatist Congregationalists as a result of the teachings of Dr. William Ames,[16] was just as intent as the Presbyterians upon retaining the collaboration between church and state which characterized the Church of England. But where the Presbyterians were content to include both the elect and the unregenerate under their wing, the Nonseparatist Congregationalists were intent upon having the elect alone join together in congregations which were to be autonomous and democratic; and, as their title indicated, not to separate from the established church.

Because of meetings held by Separatists at homes in and around Smithfield,[17] Roger Williams managed to meet followers of this most radical group of Puritans and became imbued with their doctrine of complete withdrawal from the Anglican Church, if the saints were to enjoy a pure sense of worship on earth. In 1631, the failure of the Nonseparatist Congregationalists of Massachusetts Bay to have disassociated from the Church of England was the major reason Roger Williams refused to affiliate with them, an action which led to the first breach with the Bay oligarchy.

## III  *Sir William Coke's "Soe Hopefull a Youth," 1617–1623*

The most important event in Roger's early years was his conversion, since it revealed to him the nature of God and of religion. An equally significant occurrence in his adolescence was his employment as stenographer to Sir Edward Coke,[18] England's most famous common lawyer; for this connection ultimately led to a Cambridge education and to the larger world of thought and action for which university training prepared him. It is altogether likely that had he not become associated with Coke, young Roger, like many another shopkeeper's son, might have ended up a tradesman like his father.

For the first unassailable fact of Williams' life, namely his relationship with Coke, we have the testimony of Mrs. Anne Sadleir, the lawyer's daughter: "This Roger Williams when he was a youth would in a short hand take sermons, and speeches in the Starchamber and present them to my dear father. . . ."[19] Coke, in his sixties when he employed Roger in 1617, had already become a byword in his native land for the savage manner in which he prosecuted cases of treason against the crown. Having enjoyed high office under Elizabeth, he had continued to serve her successor as Chief Justice of the Common Plea and later of the King's Bench. If cruel and vindictive to those he considered traitors, in his stand for "the liberties, franchises, privileges and jurisdictions" of his countrymen he won their respect; and, in his oft-repeated assertion that the king was not above the law, he of necessity collided with the antiquated theory of divine right upheld by James. Thrice sent to the Tower of London for actions and utterances deemed hostile to the crown, he was thrice freed; for James was unable to do without his services for very long.

Young Williams' personal development owed much to the jurist's interest in him, who "was often pleased to call me his son." A letter sent to Mrs. Sadleir in 1652 indicates this fact: "But how many thousand times . . . I had the honorable and previous remembrance of his person, and the life, the writings, the speeches, and the example of that glorious light. And . . . besides my natural inclination to study and activity, his example, instruction, and encouragement, have spurred me on to a more than ordinary, industrious and patient course in my whole course hitherto." [20]

In Coke's defiance of James's prerogative perhaps lay the genesis of Williams' later position against the Bay magistrates. In any event it was in the Star Chamber that the youthful shorthand expert learned those lessons of law and government that later stood him in good stead as the colonizer and founder of Rhode Island. Simultaneously, the summary and harsh manner in which political and religious offenders were sentenced in this room, famous for its ceiling of gilded stars, could have motivated only a deep hostility for the arbitrary power which James's officials wielded.

From Mrs. Sadleir we learn too that her father "took such liking" to his young aide "that he put him into Suttons hospital and he was the second that was placed there." Sutton's Hospital, or Charterhouse, as it afterward came to be known, was in its sixth year as a school for boys between the ages of ten and fourteen when Roger matriculated on June 25, 1621. Two years earlier its Board of Governors, of which Coke was one, had stipulated that no boys were to attend "whose parents have any Estate of Lands to leave them but onlie the Children of poor Men that want Meanes to bring them up." [21] Not poor enough to be included in the above proviso and four years older than the normal entrance age, Coke's protégé had no doubt been admitted because of his patron's influence.[22]

As with his earlier schooling, not much is known of the adolescent's two and a half year sojourn at Charterhouse, where like most grammar schools of the day, the course of study was a rigorous one, devoted almost solely to the classics. Like himself, Roger's companions were sons of "poore Men" who, in the atmosphere of piety which the school strove to inculcate, were expected to absorb the kind of education that would prepare them to act as obedient citizens of the land. Upon graduation, those Gownboys not qualified for the university were sent into the trades; those chosen for collegiate life, a selection determined by examination, were each allowed an annual pension of sixteen pounds. On July 9, 1624, the merchant taylor's son repaid Coke's faith by obtaining a scholarship to Cambridge.

## IV  *Cambridge Years, 1623–1628*

Pembroke Hall, Cambridge University, where he matriculated on June 7, 1624, was the final step in Roger's formal education. Although one of the smallest of the sixteen colleges constituting the university, Pembroke boasted a strong religious tradition; and, for matriculants like Williams who were thinking of eventually entering the ministry, it was a natural choice. Entering Cambridge as a pensioner, which meant he was financially able to pay his tuition and board, Roger automatically became a member of the group comprising the largest number of students, who together with the fellow commoners and sizars, made up the student body. Deriving mainly from middle-class families, the pensioners in an earlier day had been a distinct source of anxiety to the university officials who felt that their large influx and "rawness" would "obstruct the general progress" of the rest of the student body.[23] To understand this sense of apprehension, one has to remember that because of the great influx in the early part of the century of the sons of the wealthy tradesmen and merchants who composed the English bourgeoisie, Cambridge had been forced to modify its former aristocratic ideals of training students for law and the ministry as had previously been the case in the reigns of Henry VIII and Elizabeth.

But by the time Williams matriculated, these same pensioners had become the most influential group among the undergraduates. From their ranks, whether at Oxford or Cambridge, emerged, among others, such doughty protagonists as William Laud and Milton, both of whom like Williams became deeply immersed in the religious struggles of the age. Laud, in fact, was later to be decapitated by the Puritans for his previous efforts against them in behalf of the Anglican Church; Milton, on the other hand, was to become blind in serving the Puritan cause.

That a Cambridge education was not all that it could or should have been is seen by a quick review of its curriculum. For despite the introduction of new subjects like history, geography, and *belles-lettres* and new objectives such as the training of the whole man so that the undergraduates would leave as "young Gentlemen" who would be able to take their place in the busy world about them, the medieval trivium of rhetoric, logic, and grammar still dominated the undergraduate curriculum. Compared to the course of study in most American colleges in the 1960's, the Cambridge curriculum was an arduous one, requiring its students to rise at dawn, with the long mornings and afternoons spent in attendance with tutors or in listening to lectures. When the lectures were over, the collegians then participated both as listeners and speakers in the "public school exercises," in which constant debate, or "dialectical disputations" as they were termed, on all sorts of topics was mandatory for undergraduates seeking degrees.

Disputations and theses prepared by John Milton, who entered Christ's College in 1624, indicate the type of subject matter Williams must also have been called upon to master. Where one of Milton's disputations was on "Whether Day or Night is the more Excellent"; another dealt with the question of whether "In the Destruction of Anything there is not a Resolution of it into First Matter." Other debates were concerned with "An Attack on Scholastic Philosophy" and "On the Music of the Spheres." [24] Engaged in by students of the various colleges, these rhetorical exercises constituted the crowning test of excellence in the sense that only on the basis of their forensic skills could the young scholars expect preferment. And, while many of these disputes may have been made to order for masters of verbal fencing, the qualities of confidence, promptness, and courage which these formal discourses tended to develop in the disputants cannot be underestimated. In all of Williams' later controversies with Cotton or the Quakers, whatever else may be imputed to him, he was always immediate and sure in his arguments against them.

The ability of the university to graduate students adept in public speaking was one thing; the adherence of the administration to an antiquated curriculum like the trivium, however, disclosed a negative attitude toward the happenings of their day. For despite the introduction of the *Dialecticae* of Ramus with its heavy emphasis on reason, still the appeal to authority which the curriculum emphasized was not greatly lessened. Moreover, a fairly complete knowledge of Aristotle's works was still necessary before one could be considered a scholar.[25] As for mathematics and the astronomical discoveries of Galileo and Kepler, or even the newly formulated inductive concepts propounded by their own countryman Bacon, whose *Novum Organum* appeared in 1620, the university officials paid little attention. Nor were they interested in having the works of Jonson, Shakespeare, and the other great Elizabethan dramatists made available to their students. Bacon had in fact pleaded for a place for the new scientific thought that had evolved from the discoveries of Copernicus and Galileo. Equally vigorous was his indictment of a schooling that relied on memory instead of the reasoning faculties of the mind and on Aristotelian authority as the final source of truth.

Geared to the past and encouraging little original thinking or freedom of thought, a Cambridge education was indeed "not calculated to breed inquiring minds." [26] That inquiring minds like Milton and Williams found their schooling deficient in various ways can be seen in comments each later made. A generation after his graduation, inveighing against the kind of instruction which made undergraduates hate learning, Milton lamented that "Instead of beginning with Arts most easie," students were forced to begin with difficult "abstractions of Logick and metaphysics." [27] And while Williams honored "schooles for Tongues and Arts" which "are excellent and excell other outward gifts, as far as light excells darkness," he still referred to his college days as "monkish and idle." [28] Yet a Cambridge or an Oxford education was the only kind then available, and the argumentative training given students like Laud, Milton, and Williams served them admirably in the many controversies each was later to engage in. Still one has only to read any of Williams' controversial tracts to appreciate the serious harm this instruction did to his writing style by causing it to become crabbed and prolix; simultaneously, it enabled him to forret out weaknesses in his opponents' logic.

In retrospect, what most disturbed Williams about his collegiate years was the lack of standards and the easy acquiescence at Oxford and Cambridge to monarchal pressures: "We count the Universities the Fountaines, the Seminaries of Seedplots of all Pietie: but have not those Fountaines ever sent what streames the Times have liked and ever changed their taste and colour to the Princes eye and Palate." [29]

For it was Roger's fate to attend Cambridge in the decade in which the growing religious and political strife between the Crown and the Puritans reached its height. A university in which the majority of the students were Puritans still produced influential divines such as Lancelot Andrewes, Samuel Harsnett, and Jerome Beale, all of whom followed the Anglican doctrine laid down by Laud and served successively as masters at Pembroke. Hence it was natural that, under these circumstances, such matters of public interest as the persecutions of the Puritans and the Stuart inclination toward Catholicism should have their supporters and opponents.

In 1623, when Roger matriculated at Pembroke, events making for a greater estrangement between James I and his subjects began to accelerate, with Cambridge caught somewhere in the middle. James, anxious to replenish his dwindling treasury brought on by the demands of a luxurious and corrupt court, looked to Spanish gold as the way out of his dilemma. Consequently, in February, 1623, Prince Charles left for Spain with the avowed purpose of marrying the Infanta. As if to underline the importance of the match, when visiting Cambridge that spring James had been accompanied by the Spanish ambassador. As the months went by, the country became increasingly concerned about the outcome of the young Prince's quest, for marriage to the Infanta could restore Catholicism to the English throne.

How closely the proposed match was being followed at Cambridge is indicated in the correspondence Joseph Mede, a tutor at Christ's College, had with a former pupil, Sir Martin Stutevelle of Suffolk County. Commenting on the anxiety the populace felt about the impending marriage, Mede wrote, "This whole Spanish business is so carried in the cloudes that what effect it is like to take is not yet possible to be discerned." [30]

Meanwhile, aware of the criticism leveled against him because of his interest in Catholicism and his toleration of it, James took steps the same year to muzzle free speech and controversy, on the part of the clergy at least, by issuing his *Directions*. His pretext for its publication was that "divers young Students, by reading of late Writers and ungrounded Divines, do broach many times unprofitable, unsound seditions, and dangerous Doctrines to the scandall of the Church, and disquiet of the State, and present Government." [31]

The *Directions* made absolutely clear its primary intention that the clergy refrain from engaging in politics and adhere more closely to their own sphere of activity. In the future, no preacher was to "declare limit or bound" upon the authority of the king, or otherwise meddle in matters of state. Again, the Articles of 1562, passed in Elizabeth's reign, were to serve as guidelines to all preachers, who were not to preach any Sunday afternoon sermons "but upon some part of the Catechisme. . . ." Nor were preachers to "fall into bitter invectives and indecent railing speeches against the persons of either Papists or Puritans." On such "deep points of Predestination, Election, or Reprobation," bishops and deans alone were to hold forth. As for young men intending to enter the ministry, they were to be more carefully examined by the bishops and archbishops licensing them. All of these provisions, especially the last, would not go unminded by one matriculant at Pembroke Hall, already a Separatist in his inclination, who held serious thoughts of entering the ministry.

A test case which took place almost immediately after the *Directions* were issued indicated that James meant business about officious divines. One William Knight, an M.A. at Pembroke, in a sermon he gave at Oxford, asserted that were a person's life or chastity threatened by the civil ruler, one had the right to take up arms in self-defense. This antimonarchal stand had been previously noised abroad by a German scholar named Pareus in his "Commentary on the Romans"; repeated now by Knight, it was anathema to such as Laud and Andrewes, whose ideas about non-resistance and submission to kingly authority were in direct opposition to that of Pareus. For his pains, Knight and two of his defenders, also of Pembroke, were incarcerated, with Knight later dying from the rigors of his imprisonment.

Knight's fate had its repercussions at both Cambridge and Oxford. Following a letter by Laud, which bade divinity students adhere closely to the Scriptures for the contents of their sermons, Oxford took up the line of passive obedience to the throne; at Cambridge "the kingly power was declared to be subject to none save God, all resistance to same was pronounced infamous." [32] Furthermore, an order to burn Pareus' works at both universities was obeyed.

When Prince Charles returned home without a consort ten months after he had left, the English were jubilant; but their joy was short-lived. For in May, 1625, two months after the death of James, the young prince, now Charles I, married Henrietta Maria, a French Catholic; once again the English throne was surrounded with the trappings of Popery. And to compound the deep sense of chagrin suffered by most Englishmen, was the added realization that Charles would be just as obdurate as his father in suppressing the rights of the people in seeking to increase the power of the throne.

At this juncture, sensing that George Villiers, now Duke of Buckingham, was even more in favor with Charles than he had been with James, Parliament, comprised mainly of Puritans, proceeded to impeach him; and in June, 1626, it sent the impeachment petition to the king. To kill two birds with one stone, Charles decided to show his contempt for Parliament and to reveal the backing he had from the learned men of the nation: he installed Villiers as Chancellor of Cambridge, an office that had been left vacant by the death of Thomas Howard in May. Despite the repugnance of the Heads and students to this imposition upon them by Charles, Buckingham narrowly managed to carry the election.

In the procession held two months later at York House, where college officials, as well as undergraduate and graduate students, came to honor their newly elected Chancellor, young Williams may have been one of the participants.

In this atmosphere, therefore, of increasing hostility, Coke's protégé completed his studies and received his B.A. degree at the July commencement in 1627; but not before he had sworn to James's "three darling Articles," an action that testified his allegiance to the tenets of Anglicanism. As formulated by the late king, the three items acknowledged that the Thirty-nine Articles of Faith was agreeable to the Word of God; that the king was supreme in spiritual as well as in secular affairs; and that the Book of Common Prayer contained nothing contrary to the Word of God. Most Puritans could accept without much quibbling the validity of the Thirty-nine Articles of Faith; the acceptance of the supremacy of the king in ecclesiastical matters and of the Prayer Book as inviolate was, however, too much for many of them; and such was the case with Williams. Still his signature appears in the Cambridge subscription book of January, 1627.

In light of his future stand against oaths, Williams' signing would appear to be a temporary concession to authority. In one way it was; in another, it was not. Not to have affixed his signature would have meant the loss of a degree and nothing to show for four years of hard work; just twenty-four years old, Williams'

Separatist tendencies may also not have hardened into fixed convictions. Moreover, he may have also hoped that the established church would eventually reform some of its practices. In any event, in October, 1627, Williams began to study theology with the purpose of obtaining his M.A. Normally a three-year course, he left Cambridge about a year and a half later without completing it. In 1629, the Charterhouse records contained this entry: "Roger Williams who hath exhibition and so for about five years past, has forsaken the university and is become discontinuer of his studies there. Exhibition suspended until order to the contrary." [33]

Several factors may have gone into the divinity student's decision to leave when and as he did. He must have become increasingly aware of the inevitable clash that would ultimately take place between the king and the Puritans in the struggle for civil and religious power. In 1628, only a few months after he had started studying for his M.A., the Petition of Right was pushed through Parliament as a result of Coke's great speeches in its behalf. In August of the same year, the death by stabbing of that hated symbol of arbitrary power, the Duke of Buckingham, served as a portent of an ominous future. As Williams learned about these actions, he must have questioned the practical benefits of staying on at Cambridge, since an M.A. was not necessary to take holy orders. By this time too, his Separatist sentiments may have hardened into a firm conviction, and he must have realized it would have been well nigh impossible to keep his "soul undefiled in this point [Separatism], and not to act with a doubting conscience." [34] Moreover, Laud, now bishop of London, had instituted his system of harrying, hounding, and dismissing Nonconformist ministers from their posts, particularly Puritans; Williams must have realized it would be merely a question of time before Laud's spies caught up with him.

Last, augmenting the above reasons in a very practical way, were the two legacies left him by his father and by his uncle, Roger Pemberton, both amounting to thirty-five pounds annually, for which he was now eligible. On this amount he could live more freely than on the sixteen pounds awarded him annually by Charterhouse.

## V  *Chaplain at Otes, 1628–1630*

Sometime before February, 1629, Williams became chaplain in the household of Sir William Masham, of Otes, High Laver parish, Essex, about ten miles outside of London. Son-in-law of Sir Francis Barrington, whose daughter Elizabeth he had married, Masham, together with his father-in-law, was a member of the landed gentry, whose deep Puritan sympathies and independent political views were so characteristic of the gentry of the eastern counties For their outspoken views both men had served prison terms in 1626; again, as members of Parliament, they had defied Charles on the matter of forced loans. Sir Francis had in fact died of privations suffered during his imprisonment the summer preceding Williams' arrival at Otes.

At the Masham manor house and at Hatfield Broad Oak nearby, where Lady Joan Barrington, Sir Francis' widow lived, those militant Puritans who had been instrumental in having enacted the Petition of Right met from time to time; and, in a year or so, a good many of them would migrate to New England to escape being persecuted by both Charles and Laud. As a member of the Masham household, Williams came to know Lady Barrington, who later figured prominently in an important action he was then contemplating taking. A tough-minded, imperious woman who had accompanied her husband to prison as a matter of principle, Lady Joan brooked interference from no one and expected complete obedience from those around her, including her daughter Elizabeth, now Lady Masham, and from her two sons Thomas and Robert, who sat in Parliament for Newtown, Isle of Wight.

As a chaplain in a large manor house, Williams was expected to be on call seven days a week to minister to the spiritual welfare of all its inhabitants.[35] In practice, however, he evidently enjoyed a somewhat less strenuous life, managing to make several trips to London, one almost immediately after he had taken his new position. A letter from Robert Barrington, given to the young chaplain to deliver to Lady Joan on February, 1629, indicated that Williams, who was in London at the time, was very much aware of the savage encounters taking place between Charles and the Puritans in the third Parliament the monarch had called into session since his accession.[36] Within three weeks of Barrington's letter,

Parliament had been dismissed, but not before it had pushed through the *Remonstrance,* which proclaimed as traitors to the liberties of England those who encouraged the innovation of either Popery or Arminianism so much favored by Laud and the king or advised the levying of Tonnage and Poundage without grant of Parliament.

The *Remonstrance* was the last act passed by Parliament before it was dismissed by Charles for a period of eleven years. Of the doings on that memorable March 2 in 1620, when the act was passed, Roger Williams was a spectator, since Thomas Barrington wrote to his mother that, "What the particulars were, you have an eye witness to report at your leisure." [37] What the young chaplain's feelings were as he saw the detested policies of Charles and Laud suffer a momentary defeat is not known. But the repressive measures the king and his archbishop soon laid on the leaders of Parliament certainly alerted him that time had indeed run out for any real healing of the breach between the Puritans and the throne.

Williams' stay in the Masham manor at Otes, however, was not completely taken up by his activities as a spiritual adviser and as an observer of history in-the-making. This is seen in two letters he wrote Lady Barrington in the late spring of 1629;[38] for their contents reveal that Williams, now twenty-five, had fallen in love with and wished to marry Lady Joan's niece, Jane Whalley. But because of his background as a tradesman's son, Roger's suit was repulsed by the aunt, who apparently sought a suitor from a higher social level. Despite a serious illness suffered as a consequence of his rejection, the young clergyman soon recovered and found love elsewhere. For an entry in the parish of High Laver dated December 15, 1629 read that: "Roger Williams clarke and Mary Barnard were married." [39]

Before her betrothal to Williams, Mary Barnard had served as maid or companion to Jug Altham, Lady Masham's daughter by a previous marriage. Although the daughter of Richard Barnard, a minister from Nottinghamshire and a well-known figure in his own day because of the many books he had written, Mary herself was unlettered. Still, the marriage must have been a happy one since Williams referred to her as a "deare wife" and in 1652 wrote his *Experiments of Spiritual Life and Health* to lift her from a state of spiritual despondency.

In his letters to Lady Joan asking for her niece's hand, the ardent suitor had mentioned as one of his prospects a "late New England call," a credible prospect in light of the growing number of settlements springing up in the New World. Seeing no hope of a cessation of the punitive measures constantly being enacted against them, the Puritans of the eastern counties of England had turned their thoughts to New England as a means of escape. For this purpose a group of them in 1628 had bought land from the Council of New England and had dispatched John Endecott to Salem. A charter granted on March 4, 1629, by the king to the Massachusetts Bay Company, as the emigration-minded Puritans were now known, was the basis for a meeting in August of the same year at Sempringham, Lincolnshire. There plans were worked out for the sailing, the following March, of eleven ships with seven hundred passengers who would settle at Massachusetts Bay with John Winthrop as governor.

Williams met Winthrop at this midsummer meeting, and while en route to the assembly he had also become acquainted with Thomas Hooker and John Cotton, two other ministers who later played important roles in the development of New England. An entry some sixteen years later indicates how differently Williams had already begun to feel while at Otes about upholding one of the "three darling articles" he had sworn to at Cambridge: "Master Cotton may call to minde, that the discusser riding with himself and one other of precious memorie, Master Hooker to and from Sempringham presented his arguments from Scripture why he durst not joyn with them in their use of Common Prayer." [40]

It was with Cotton, after the latter had arrived in New England in 1633 and had become the teacher of the Boston church and then the leading exponent of the New England Way, that Williams clashed head-on. This controversy led to the tracts both of them later wrote to defend their respective positions on separation versus nonseparation from the Anglican Church.

With Laud's harassment of nonconforming ministers continually being accelerated, it was only a matter of time before Williams would lose his post at Otes.[41] Again, with the departure of the Massachusetts Bay colonists in March, 1630, fresh in mind, the "late New England call" must have appeared to be the only practical resolution of the predicament of the recently married Separatist and his wife. Furthermore, the Massachusetts Bay colonists had given as the primary reason for their emigration the conversion of the Indians. To Williams, whose "soul's desire was to do the natives good," [42] the opportunity to bring Christianity to the savages must have been the final inducement to leave England. On December 10, 1630, Roger and Mary Williams sailed for America from Bristol on the *Lyon*.

CHAPTER *2*

# Roger Williams in New England

TO THE virgin forest land of New England, inhabited by wild animals, Indians, and newly settled Englishmen, nearly all of whom had fled the mother country to escape religious persecution, Williams brought the Separatist notions he had entertained in England. Because of these unorthodox ideas and similar ones he held concerning the roles of church and state, he was forced within the space of five years to change his place of residence four times before he was eventually exiled. In founding Providence shortly after his exile, primarily for victims of religious persecution, and in later helping other exiles from the Bay to build the colony of Rhode Island, Williams became engaged in a task that took almost a half century and the maturest years of his life.

That the tiny settlements around Narragansett Bay managed to remain together, despite centrifugal pressures placed upon them by arch individualists like William Harris, William Coddington, Anne Hutchinson, and Samuel Gorton, was a testimony to Williams' faith and that of others like him, who regarded the colony as a new political and religious "deal" for transplanted Europeans. Other pressures were there too and these came mostly from the Bay, who sought either to swallow up the tiny towns or to place them under her own jurisdiction. That Providence Plantations, as the tiny settlements were first called, managed to surmount these inner and outer pressures and become a legitimate colony in their own right was the result not only of faith but also of great sacrifices, hardships, and outlays of money and time on the part of Williams. His efforts to consolidate and preserve the independence of Rhode Island included trips to England in 1643 and in 1651: the first, to obtain a charter for the beleaguered settlements; the second, to confirm the charter originally given recognizing Providence Plantations as a colony.

Founding Providence had not been Williams' original intention. Building a trading post and converting the Narragansett Indians had been; but, once the town was founded, it was to be one where the inhabitants were to enjoy "liberty and equality, both in land and government." [1] In this blueprint of the type of colony he meant Providence to be, Williams was indeed a visionary. For this utopian dream was a difficult matter to bring to fruition in a new continent where immigrants brought with them keen remembrances of the aristocratic role the possession of large tracts of land played in the mother country. For a time, however, Williams' provision coupling the possesion of land with the right to vote kept the early land-hungry settlers of Providence in line. But, almost from the outset, the trend was against economic and political democracy; and Williams' efforts to insure a sense of fairness and justice in these two areas to the incoming settlers were eroded. He lived in fact to witness the day when private land companies, the *modus operandi* in other New England colonies, sprang up in the towns of Rhode Island. Under this regimen those settlers already holding property had the undivided town lands pass into their possession, thus insuring the denial of tracts of land to future residents.[2]

If his efforts for political and economic democracy fell through, the idea of religious liberty, for which he became justly famous, more than prevailed. From its very inception, Providence, and later the other Rhode Island settlements, became the sanctuaries for both those who were banished from the Bay and for others harboring various unorthodox beliefs which they wished to be left free to practice. As Winthrop put it, "At their first coming thither, Mr. Williams and the rest did make an order, that no man should be molested for his conscience." [3] And from the outset, Separatists, Seekers, and Baptists were among the earliest settlers of Providence. In 1683 Antinomians founded Portsmouth; in the 1650's Jews from different parts of the world were allowed to enter the colony, as were the Quakers. In short, any sect was sure of finding sanctuary as long as its members obeyed the civil laws of the various settlements.

Hence Williams must have been immeasurably thrilled when the charter granted the colony in 1663 by Charles II contained one provision insuring absolute freedom of conscience to all its settlers. At a time when such freedom had not yet been granted

native-born English dissenters in the mother country and when
Massachusetts and Connecticut still maintained a rigid orthodoxy
over its inhabitants, this legal guarantee of religious freedom
owed much to Williams and his successful application of the idea
in Providence. Left to grow on its vigorous own, this concept of
religious liberty became so much part of American religious thinking that the free exercise of one's faith without interference was
incorporated in 1791 into the Bill of Rights.

To defend the position that the Bay orthodoxy took about what
they deemed to be Williams' unsettling and perverse ideas, both
their early and later historians such as William Hubbard, Nathaniel Morton, and Cotton Mather wrote caustically about their an-
tagonist.[4] Read in the context of our times, their utterances damn
them more than they do their adversary. Yet interestingly enough,
they never vilified Williams' personal or moral character, despite
the fact that their purposes would have been served admirably
had they been able to impute execrable and devilish motives to a
person of immoral background. As an individual, Williams won
the respect and admiration of all those who really got to know
him both in old and New England; indeed, two of the more important members of the orthodoxy, Winthrop and William Bradford, governors of Massachusetts Bay and Plymouth respectively,
thought very highly of him until his religious and political ideas
clashed with theirs.[5]

Still it was not only men of his own race and of a similar religious background who respected Williams' sterling character; the
Narragansetts and other Indian tribes whom he got to know
through his trading and early missionary activities also admired
him. Because of the affection borne him by Canonicus and Mian-
tunomi, two Sachems of the Narragansetts, Williams was literally
given the land which served as the site of Providence. As for his
efforts in helping to keep the peace among the various Indian
tribes themselves, and between the Narragansetts and the Bay
colonists who were intent upon defrauding the natives of their
land, not enough praise can be bestowed upon the man. Almost
singlehandedly, his endeavors as a peacemaker—both after he
had been banished and later whenever his abilities as a negotiator
and translator were called upon—made possible the growth and
permanence of the small English colonies.

Between the Pequot War of 1636 and King Philip's War in

1675, there were, to be sure, forays against the English settlements; but these were relatively few and sporadic in nature. That
there were a minimum of Indian attacks against the colonial settlements during these years was due in good measure to Williams'
many exertions as a negotiator between the Indians and the settlers. Yet for his many efforts to prevent war between the Narragansetts and the English, Williams was only perfunctorily
thanked by the Bay leaders. Behind their coolness toward the man
who worked so vigorously in their behalf lay a great sense of hostility, which existed almost from the time Williams set foot on
New England soil. The reasons for this estrangement must now be
considered.

## I Trouble with the Bay Oligarchy, 1631–1635

According to Winthrop, Roger Williams and his wife Mary arrived at Nantasket, just outside Boston, on February 5, 1631.[6] The
facts concerning Williams' immediate and continuing alienation
from the Bay orthodoxy for the next five years are well known and
can be rapidly related. Tendered the post of teacher at the church
in Boston, an enviable assignment for any young, ambitious minister, Williams declined to become affiliated with the Nonseparatist
Congregationalists because, as he stated, he "durst not officiate to
an unseparated people." [7] When next offered the office of assistant to Reverend Samuel Skelton on April 12, at Salem, he accepted. But, before leaving Boston, he had "declared his opinion"
that the magistrates were acting outside their jurisdiction in punishing breaches "of the Sabbath . . . as it was a breach of the
first table." [8] As this table referred to the first four of the Ten
Commandments, which dealt with man's duties and responsibilities to God, Williams was in effect insisting that the magistrate
was acting outside his rightful sphere in punishing matters dealing with conscience. Here was the Separatist's first pronounce-
ment of separation in a new area: that of church and state and
their respective spheres of influence.

No wonder Winthrop "marvelled" that Salem "would choose
him without advising with the council." Despite Salem's "initial
refusal to forbear to proceed till they had conferred about it,"
Governor Endecott and his colony eventually submitted to the
pressure put upon them by the Bay; and, after a stay of just a few

months, Williams was forced to leave Salem. Plymouth Colony, settled in 1620 by the Pilgrims, was the next place of residence for him, who had probably begun to feel the same sense of harassment in New England that he had suffered under Laud in the mother country. From 1631 to 1633 Williams served as assistant to Ralph Smith, the Plymouth pastor, and had frequent opportunities to teach and preach to the congregation who, while Separatists like himself, yet allowed no other worship in the colony but their own.

Warmly regarded by Bradford and other Pilgrim officials upon his arrival, Williams soon became *persona non grata* because of a treatise he had written at Bradford's request in which he asserted that the Plymouth patent, recently extended by Charles I, was invalid; no kings, wrote Williams, including Charles, were "invested with Right by virtue of their Christianitie to take and give away the Lands and Countries of other men." [9] This idea that the lands of the New World belonged by right to the native inhabitants, was of course, diametrically opposed to the then commonly accepted theory that all tracts of land discovered in the name of the European monarchs automatically became their property. Thus to be told they had no right to the land they were living on was too much of a pill for the Pilgrims to swallow. From this time forth Bradford, who had initially considered Williams a godly and zealous man, worked for his removal from Plymouth.

Besides offering Williams and his wife a temporary abode, the Plymouth sojourn was important in another respect. In his two years there Williams learned the rigorous facts of colonial life: he supported his family by working alternately as a preacher and as a farmer, and served simultaneously as a trader and a missionary among the Indians whose dialects he had begun to master. Concern for the rights of the natives, who were being divested of their lands by the English settlers, had in fact, motivated the treatise impugning the validity of the charter.

Dismissed from his Plymouth post in August, 1633, Williams returned to Salem to serve again as assistant to Reverend Skelton. By November he was differing once more with the Bay colonists, this time with their efforts to impose its hegemony over the churches in the entire colony. In their efforts to do so, the Bay ministers and those of Saugus had met on a fortnightly basis, according to Winthrop to debate "some question of moment."

Warned by his experience of two years before, when he had attacked magisterial incursions into matters of faith, Williams saw in these biweekly meetings an attempt to impose the same kind of uniformity and centralization of church discipline that Laud had previously prescribed in England. Both Skelton and he objected to these ministerial assemblies "fearing . . . [they] might grow in time to a presbytery or superintendency to the prejudice of the churches' liberties." In 1637, four years later, what both Salem ministers feared came to pass. A synod held at Newton at that time, allowing for magisterial enforcement of the first table, with the magistrates to be "open" for advice from their ministers, did in fact establish a "superintendency" over the churches in the Bay area. Yet in 1633, Winthrop could still write that Williams' "fear was without cause; for they were all clear in that point that no church . . . can have power over another church." [10]

But concern with the establishment of a presbytery was child's play compared to an entry of a more serious nature in Winthrop's journal on December 27. Understandably disturbed by the "strange opinions" concerning the need for rigid separation voiced by Williams at Plymouth, Bradford had previously felt it necessary to warn Salem "concerning him and what care they ought to have of him." [11] Alert to the admonition, Winthrop asked Williams for a copy of his treatise, which was duly forwarded. Examining the document, Winthrop and his assistants found exasperating both the statement disputing "their right to the lands they possessed here," and the author's conclusion that, "claiming by the king's grant, they could have no title, nor otherwise except they compounded with the natives." Williams' sentiments could not have been uttered at a more unpropitious time; for, because of their enemies, the Bay colonists had begun to fear the revocation of its charter and the subsequent installation of a royal governor. Charles needed only to overhear ideas such as these challenging his authority and the Bay charter would surely have been revoked.

Three passages in the treatise particularly provoked the Bay officials. In one Williams called King James a liar, "because in his patent he blessed God that he was the first Christian prince that had discovered this land"; a second clause charged James "with blasphemy for calling Europe Christendom, or the Christian world"; the most damaging, though, was the third one in which

Williams used three uncomplimentary passages from the Book of Revelation to "personally apply to our present king, Charles." Denunciation of the Stuarts or of any persons he deemed wrongdoers was characteristic of Williams when he was certain of his moral position. Furthermore, a sense of prudence in withholding accusations like the above for a more favorable time was totally against his nature. If a moral principle were involved, a so-called right or wrong time played no factor in his decision to have his say. It is to his credit that, being of an ardent and impulsive nature, he was almost always on the side of the angels on those principles that truly civilized nations have come to live by.

For Williams' denial of the king's patent and at the advice of some of the "most judicious ministers who much condemned Mr. Williams' error and presumption," the Bay council ordered Williams to be present at the next court where he was to be censured. Advised to retract his statements, Williams replied in a submissive manner that his sole intention in having written the treatise was for Bradford's "private satisfaction." For all he cared, Winthrop could burn the paper.[12] Prior to the convening of the next court on March 4, 1634, at which time "he appeared penitently, and gave satisfaction of his intention and loyalty," the council had met on January 24 to consider the treatise which they did not find "to be so evil as at first . . . seemed." If Williams retracted or took an oath of allegiance to the king, the intended rebuke against him would therefore be dismissed.[13] Since he evidently complied with this request, the council abstained from censuring him. As things turned out, the matter of the revocation of the grant was to come up again; before a year had elapsed, Williams was accused of having "broken his promise" in having spoken in public against the king's patent and "for terming the churches of England antichristian." [14] The latter charge of course stemmed from his ardent stand for Separatism.

To further compound his role as a troublemaker in the Puritan Zion, Williams took an emphatic stand against the "resident's oath" enacted by the Bay magistrates in April, 1634, to ensure the loyalty of all its settlers against any eventual conflict with the crown. Williams, acting on the conviction that an oath was purely a spiritual matter—a "part of God's worship, and God's worship was not to be put on carnall persons"—was so vehement in his opposition that the court was unable to enforce the measure. Had the oath been enforced, the residents of the Bay area would have in effect sworn allegiance to the "lawes and constitucions of the colony" to which they would have to be "obedient and comformable." [15] So far had the Bay oligarchy been prepared to go in order to supersede the provision in their charter pledging loyalty to the King and England's laws!

By March, 1635, the magistrates had substituted an "Oath of Fidelity" to replace the one which Williams' earlier opposition had made inoperative. Simultaneously, the magistrates had asked for a uniform church discipline and for a consideration of "how far the magistrates are bound to interpose" for this discipline to take effect. Because this union of civil and church power attempted to impose conformity and struck at the heart of independent Congregationalism, Williams denounced the proposed request. As a result of these various differences, the oligarchy thought the time favorable by July 8 for a showdown with Williams. His defiance of the magistrates' enactments made it imperative that Williams be stopped for good; if he were not, they would have to forego the idea that they had any authority. Summoned to court on that date, he was indicted on four counts, only two of which were serious: his having asserted that magistrates were out of order in punishing breaches of the first table, and that they "ought not to tender an oath to an unregenerate man." [16]

The magistrates and ministers judged Williams' opinions "to be erroneous and very dangerous," and he and the Salem church were given until the convening of the next general court to think matters over; at that time they were expected "to give satisfaction to the court or else expect the sentence." Another factor that served to congeal Bay resentment against Williams had been Salem's recent appointment of him as their pastor eight months after Skelton's death in August, 1634; this action Winthrop regarded as "a great contempt of authority." For their temerity in having acted in a manner wholly consistent with independent Congregationalism, Salem was denied land in Marblehead Neck which rightfully belonged to it. The immediate reaction of the Salem congregation at being deprived of its property was to write "to other churches to admonish the magistrates of this as a heinous sin." The Bay reaction was to exclude the Salem deputies at the next general court "until they should give satisfaction about the letter." [17]

In addition to having been the motivating force behind the
letter sent out by the Salem church, Williams also penned a stiff
note of protest to the elders of Boston to condemn their refusal to
turn over the land in question as an example of dealing "with a
church out of a church way." *A Model of Church and Civil Power*,
a tract drawn up at this time by various ministers of the Bay and
soon dispatched to Salem for the edification of its inhabitants, left
no doubt about the Bay position. The first written document of
the New England Way in church and state, the *Model* made it
clear that magistrates had the right to intervene in church disputes if these tended to schisms or separation. Sensing the pressure being put on his townsmen to leave him in the lurch, Williams, then ill, wrote in August to his church that he could no
longer "communicate with the churches in the Bay; neither would
he communicate with them except they would refuse communion
with the rest." [18] This step, to separate from the rest of the Bay
churches, the Salem congregation was not prepared to follow. As
a result, Williams no longer held services in the Salem church;
instead, he held meetings in his home, the small group comprised
mostly of women. In holding services in his own home, Williams
was practicing separation in its most literal sense.

In the meantime, the Salem settlement had been given to
understand that the land at Marblehead Neck would be theirs if it
went along with the Bay in its censure of Williams. Thus, after
alienating many of his townspeople, the Bay magistrates felt the
time had come once and for all to stop their Separatist pastor.
October 8 was the date set for his next appearance in court; and
the accusation was his having left his ministry at Salem. It was no
ordinary assemblage that gathered for the General Court session
at the Newtown church on that date. Besides "all the ministers in
the Bay being desired to be present," present also were the magistrates and their assistants; presiding over the whole body was
Governor Haynes.

Williams was "charged with the said two letters," the first to the
churches which had rebuked the action of the Bay magistrates in
withholding the land as a "heinous sin"; the second to his own
church urging separation from the Bay churches, whom, because
of their nonseparation from the Church of England, he had termed
"full of anti-christian pollution." When called upon to answer,
Williams not only justified the two letters but "maintained all his

opinions." Given the alternative to have his ideas presently disputed or to enjoy a month's respite to think over his position, he chose instead to dispute. Oddly enough, the person chosen as his disputant was Thomas Hooker, who with Cotton had arrived in New England in 1633. Within a year after Williams' trial, Hooker would leave his own pastorate at Newtown to become the chief founder of Hartford, Connecticut, because of a conflict with Cotton on matters of doctrine. Governor Haynes, too, would later have "some difference with the Bay" and depart for Hartford to take up residence. But in the fall of 1635, Hooker and Haynes were still affiliated with the theocracy; and, despite Hooker's efforts to have Williams change his views, he failed in the attempt.

The court's reaction to Williams' obstinacy was swift, and on the following day sentence was given. Because he had "broached & dyvulged dyvers newe & dangerous opinions, against the authoritie of magistrates . . . & yet mainetaineth the same without retraccòn," Williams was commanded to "dep(ar)te out of this jurisdiccòn within six weekes." Failure to heed this expulsion order would be sufficient cause for the magistrates "to send him to some place out of this jurisdiction. . . ." [19]

Reams have been written since 1635 by both admirers and detractors of Williams, either denouncing or upholding the sentence imposed by the court. His admirers saw Williams as being punished primarily for conscience' sake, while his detractors regarded him as being judged solely for acts committed against duly constituted authority. For a better understanding of these two positions, it is necessary to examine the specific charges made against Williams. The four charges levied against him by the magistrates, to which Williams later agreed that "the particulars were rightly summed up," [20] were as follows: the Indians and not the colonists were "the true owners" of the land; it was unlawful for a wicked person to engage in "actions of Gods worship" or for anyone to "heare any of the Ministers of the Parish Assemblies in England"; and last, the jurisdiction of the civil magistrates extended no further than "to the Bodies and Goods, and outward state of men."

The major indictments were, of course, first his impugning the Bay's right to the land "by Pattent from the King," and second his desire to restrict the duties of the magistrates to their civil sphere of duty. These two positions divorced Williams from any consid-

eration of sympathy from the Bay judiciary; to them he was striking at the very right of the colonists to be in North America in the
first place, as well as calling into question the validity of the commonwealth that the Puritans had built in the wilderness. And, in
reiterating Luther's claim that the legal power of the magistrates
reached only to the bodies and property of their subjects, Williams was in direct opposition to the *Model of Church and Civil
Power*, which had given the magistrates the right to interfere in
spiritual matters. In this sense, then, it can be said that Williams
was defying duly constituted authority. But in maintaining his
stand that the magistrate's office was a purely civil one, he was
indeed being punished for conscience' sake.

At bottom, the real split between Williams and the Bay lay in
their different approaches to Bible history. Where Winthrop, Cotton, and the other Bay Puritans viewed themselves as latter-day
Hebrews building a New Jerusalem in a new world and had accordingly patterned a theocracy similar to that of their biblical
predecessors, Williams viewed the Bay commonwealth as an un-
true state of affairs because of the Christian dispensation. And far
from the church being the dominant institution in any city or settlement, as had been the case in the Middle Ages, and a course
which the oligarchy was intent upon pursuing, Williams, as we
shall see, viewed any church and its members as merely a private
organization with no more rights than that accorded to any other
private company or group.[21]

As for the other two charges—the fitness of those engaged in
worship, and the propriety of colonists' hearing Anglican ministers
on visits to the mother country—these were doctrinal points on
which there could be honest differences of opinion, depending on
one's Separatist or Nonseparatist views.

Originally ordered to depart within six weeks, Williams might
have remained in Salem until the following spring, his sentence
having been stayed because of poor health. He might have, but
Williams being Williams, the magistrates soon learned that, despite the warning given him not to express his views, "he did use
to entertain company in his house, and to preach to them, even of
such points as he had been censured for." [22] Warned by Winthrop
that the magistrates meant to apprehend him, Williams fled Salem
for Narragansett country early in January, 1636.

## II *Founding and Growth of Rhode Island, 1636–1657*

In removing to southwestern Narrangansett territory, which lay outside the Bay patent, Williams was following a preconceived plan. In talks he had had with Winthrop long before his banishment, Williams had agreed with his older friend that this area was a most likely place to build a trading post both as a base for his trading activities with the Indians as well as a station for furthering their conversion. But in January, 1636, when he was literally running for his life in a season of bitter cold, the immediate objective was to stay alive. To that end he first found refuge in the "filthy smoke holes" of the Wampanoags whom he had befriended while at Plymouth. By May, after a false start in founding a colony at Seekonk, which lay within the Plymouth patent, Williams and four others who joined him that spring founded Providence on a site whose land he had purchased from Canonicus, the head sachem of the Narragansetts. Like Sir Edward Coke before him, the old Indian leader also thought of Williams as a son.[23]

If a trading station had originally been Williams' plan in removing to the Narragansett country, he had evidently changed his mind even before he quit Salem. For, according to Winthrop, the chief reason the Bay magistrates were intent upon apprehending Williams before he fled was that he had infected "above twenty persons" in Salem with his heterodox ideas. These dissenters now meant to join him in erecting a plantation about the Narragansett Bay, "from whence the infection would easily spread into these churches." How truly devout Williams' character must have been is seen in Winthrop's concluding remark that "many of them [were] much taken with the apprehension of his godliness." [24]

To the Bay, Williams' intention of starting a plantation meant the extension of heresy and its propagation outside the borders of Massachusetts, an action that needed to be stopped immediately. Of dissenters, other than Williams, who were growing increasingly bold and resentful of the Bay's use of compulsion to forward a strict conformity, the oligarchs were beginning to get their fill. About a year after Williams had fled, the brethren had their hands full with the "erroneous opinions" of Anne Hutchinson and the others associated with her in the Antonomian heresy. This remarkable woman, who had left England expressly to follow the teachings of her minister John Cotton in New England, nearly proved to be his undoing because of her belief that truth could be obtained by inner revelation, a doctrine with which Cotton for a time agreed until pressured by his Bay brethren to recant.

Still the Bay's efforts to suppress heresy both inside and outside its borders were to prove gradually ineffective. The Reformation with its emphasis on each man being his own prophet had gone too far in leavening human thought to have mass conformity succeed. For those who felt hemmed in by Bay intolerance, there was always an escape elsewhere. It was with this thought in mind that Williams "agreed that the place [Providence] should be for such as were destitute especially for Conscience sake. . . ." [25] The treatment and sentence accorded him by the magistrates had opened his eyes to the need for a plantation to serve as a place of refuge for others who, like himself, would be either punished or banished by the orthodox for their heterodox beliefs. To guarantee this liberty of conscience, in the revised political compact drawn up by the settlers of Providence in 1639, was added the phrase "only in civil things," [26] thus insuring that future town governments would be restricted solely to matters of a civil nature. Thus came about the first practical application on American soil of the principle of separation of church and state.

In a letter to Winthrop[27] soon after Providence had been founded, Williams told how its inhabitants had agreed to a democratic form of government based on the same plan of mutual agreement which had characterized the proceedings of the Pilgrims in the Mayflower *Compact*. By June 16, "masters of families" were meeting every two weeks and consulting about their "common peace, watch, and planting," and with "mutual consent" they were able to finish "all matters with speed and peace."

Aside from establishing Providence as a haven for religious refugees, Williams meant to institute a political democracy in which latecomers were to have the same equal rights to the purchase of land as the early settlers; furthermore, suffrage was to be extended to all householders and masters of families. That equal rights in the purchase of Providence plots went into effect directly is seen by the testimony of William Harris, one of the original five settlers, who claimed that he and the three others were "actually and immediately" given "equal possession" of the land with Wil-

liams by purchase.[28] The intention of land allotment mentioned
above was drawn up in 1638 and was known as the Initial Deed.
In it Williams made over "Equall Right in Injoying and dispossing
the Same grounds and lands unto my loveing Friends and Neigh-
bours and Such others as the Major part of us shall admitt unto
the same fellowship of Vote with us." [29]

Meant to guarantee, insofar as one person's efforts could, uniformity of land ownership and suffrage, Williams' equalitarian political and economic views were soon discarded by the early settlers who, led by Harris, in their greedy desire for large tracts of
land, soon negated their founder's idealistic plans. Yet, desirous as
he was for political and economic democracy to obtain, Williams
was by no means a social democrat in the sense that his colony
was open to everyone. In the letter mentioned to Winthrop above,
he had declared "That as I freely subject myself to common consent, and shall not bring in any person into the town without their
consent; so also that against my consent no person be violently
brought in and received." [30]

Despite this assertion, there is no evidence he ever took action
to prevent anyone from settling in the colony he had founded. Considering some of the rabble to whom Providence and the other
settlements in Providence Plantations eventually gave sanctuary,
and the troubles caused by religious malcontents, who for the
most part mistook liberty of conscience for license, Williams expressed great forbearance in never pressing for legislation to exclude anyone seeking shelter there. Certainly the provocation to
do just that presented itself many times.

Besides Providence, other settlements in the area of Narragansett Bay were founded by victims of the Bay magistrates. As a
result of the Antinomian controversy of 1637, which led to the
banishment of Anne Hutchinson and her group, Williams was instrumental in having these latest victims of persecution take up
residence in Aquidneck, the large island in Narragansett Bay
which he had bought from Canonicus for William Coddington,
their leader. By spring, 1639, the Antinomians founded Portsmouth at the northernmost tip of Aquidneck. Soon thereafter religious and political differences broke out between Coddington and
the Hutchinsons, with the latter faction aided by the ubiquitous
Samuel Gorton, who was already notorious for his impugning all

magisterial enactments not based on English common law. Soon Coddington and his followers were deposed; in no way fazed, they founded Newport at the southern end of Aquidneck.

Anxious to form a settlement of his own, one distinct from that of Providence, Coddington managed by 1640 to join Portsmouth and Newport into a single combination which lasted until 1647. This union, however, did not afford settlers the same political rights enjoyed by their Providence neighbors, for Coddington had a feudal sense of government; still no one in his federation was to be reckoned a "Delinquent" for "Doctrine," so firmly entrenched had the concept of absolute religious freedom become, thanks to Williams and the example of Providence.

In 1641, Gorton, whom Coddington had banished from Portsmouth because of his opposition to the federation of the previous year, sought refuge in Providence. While freely allowed to enter the town, he and his followers were denied the right to become permanent residents because of the notoriety accorded their past actions, nearly all of which were motivated by Gorton's flaming desire to have all colonial legislation predicated on the common law of England. Because of these efforts to protect the civil rights of his fellow English colonists, Gorton and his supporters had been previously hounded by the Bay and Connecticut magistrates who were not at all interested in dissociating civil authority from the religious sphere. The Gortonists finally found refuge in Warwick in 1643, but even there they were harried by the Bay magistrates until they finally obtained the protection of English law in 1646.[31] In the short time he spent at Providence, Gorton proved a thorn in the side of its settlers, converting a number of the townspeople to his way of thinking, while, according to Williams, simultaneously "bewitching and bemadding poor Providence."

By 1643, the time had come to obtain a charter to unite the straggling settlements and to halt the tendency toward anarchy which had come in the wake of actions taken by such strong individualists as Coddington, Harris, and Gorton. Another incentive to obtain a patent was the premeditated exclusion of Rhode Island the same year from the newly formed New England Confederacy, an act which posed a threat to the existence of the various Narragansett settlements. Furthermore, since the titles of these small towns were based on Indian land deeds, the Bay and Con-

necticut magistrates felt no obligation to honor them, acting as
they did from the premise that all of North America belonged to
the English by virtue of Cabot's discovery. That the Narragansett
area lay outside the boundaries of their respective charters did not
in the least disturb the Bay or Connecticut officials, intent as they
were on either destroying Rhode Island or putting its towns and
inhabitants under their respective jurisdictions. For, in serving as
a haven for all types of disaffected religionists, as well as Jews and
Quakers, Rhode Island was considered a disgrace to the "more
godly citizens" of the Bay and Connecticut.

Added to the above reasons for obtaining a charter were such
enemies in their midst as William Arnold, one of the early settlers
of Providence, who sought to place Pawtuxet, founded in 1638 as
an offshoot of Providence, under the jurisdiction of Massachusetts.
Hence in March, 1643, Williams sailed for England; there after
waiting more than a year, a situation occasioned by the outbreak
of the Civil War between Charles and the Puritans, he obtained
his patent. During his approximately fifteen months abroad, Williams found time among other activities to write some of his more
important controversial works, including his most famous one,
*The Bloudy Tenent of Persecution.*

In September, 1644, he was back in Providence with his patent,
which authorized the incorporation of Providence, Portsmouth,
and Newport under the title of Providence Plantations.[32] Interestingly enough, the patent allowed for the formation of whatever
type of civil government its inhabitants desired; simultaneously it
afforded the civil authorites no control over church affairs.[33] In
short, the separation of church and state had actually become law
for Rhode Island. Yet, despite these favorable provisions, ten
years were to elapse and the charter had to be reconfirmed before
Rhode Island could become a united colony. In the first place, the
1644 patent could not be put into effect immediately because of
Coddington's earlier union of Portsmouth and Newport. In 1647,
however, Portsmouth revoked her tie with her sister town and
held a general assembly at which freemen from the various settlements including Warwick voted into being a federal government
possessing centralized powers. While the four towns retained their
corporate rights, legal and political control was vested in a general
assembly. But this union did not last long; Coddington, unhappy

at the formation of a united Rhode Island, obtained a commission in 1651 from the Council of State in England which made him governor for life of Aquidneck. This appointment in effect nullified the charter obtained seven years earlier by Williams.

To revoke the commission granted Coddington and to ratify the 1644 patent, Williams and John Clarke sailed for England in November, 1651. There, despite many months of waiting, necessitated in large part by Cromwell's domestic and foreign problems, Williams was successful in obtaining the specific objectives for which he had sailed. When not busy negotiating for the confirmation of his patent, he kept busy writing and publishing works emphasizing the necessity for absolute religious freedom, including *The Bloody Tenent Yet More Bloody;* simultaneously he attacked the position of those in old and New England who sought to deny what to him was a fundamental human right.

On his return to Providence in 1654, from which he had been away for two and a half years, Williams found Rhode Island and its inhabitants more disorganized and more at odds than they had ever been. The Arnolds were still plotting the annexation of Pawtuxet to the Bay; Coddington entertained no idea of submitting to the authority of the newly confirmed charter until he had to; and William Harris, an astute lawyer, was beginning to add the idea of anarchy to his numerous other schemes for forestalling unity in the colony.

Elected president of the general assembly in September, 1654, Williams at last had the opportunity to take the necessary steps to subdue the factious groups and to bring order and stability out of dissension. Just prior to his taking office, amazed at the unbridled individualism and license of his townsmen, he was led to write how he felt about their lack of restraint.[34] Claiming he was "like a man in a great fog," who knew "not well how to steer," Williams reminded them of the many sacrifices he had made in their behalf, sacrifices which had resulted in their not having become "enslaved to the bondages . . . of . . . both soul and body oppressions of the English and the barbarians about us." The letter had a salutary effect; Providence agreed to meet with her three sister settlements to openly discuss their differences; a letter from Cromwell, written March 29, 1655, also immeasurably heartened Williams. Counseling the Rhode Islanders to get on with the process of governing themselves as granted them in their charter, the Lord Protector admonished the settlers not to allow "any intestine commotions or forraigne invasions" to bring "any detriment or dishonour to the Commonwealth or yourselves as farr as you by your care and diligence can prevent." [35]

In his three years as president of Rhode Island, 1654–57, several problems arose which gave Williams an opportunity to demonstrate his political acumen in handling two of the colony's chief faults: the unwarranted freedom of speech and the uncontrolled individualism of the inhabitants. One such case, in November, 1654, dealt with the refusal of some conscientious objectors of the Baptist faith to bear arms for the defense of the colony. However, while simultaneously protesting against military duty, these objectors were also busy circulating a paper asserting it to be "bloodguiltiness, and against the rule of the gospel, to execute judgement upon transgressors, against the private or public weal." [36]

Sensing in their refusal to perform militia service not a deep conviction for pacificism but a tendency toward anarchy, Williams' response was to pen the justly famous letter in which the role of a government toward its citizens was compared to that of a ship and its passengers. Decrying the idea that his thought had ever been so misjudged as to stand for "an infinite liberty of conscience," Williams once again aired his views on the difference between freedom of worship and civil liberty, which he had elaborated upon ten years previously in *The Bloudy Tenent*. The passengers, whether "papists, protestants, Jews and Turks," were not to "be forced to come to the ships' prayers of worship, nor compelled from their own particular prayers or worship, if they practice any." By it was to be understood that "the commander of this ship ought to command the ship's course" and should

any seaman refuse to perform their services, or passengers to pay their freight; if any refuse to help, in person or purse, towards the common charges or defence; if any refuse to obey the common laws and orders of the ship, concerning their common peace or preservation, if any shall mutiny and rise up against their commanders and officers; if any should preach or write that there ought to be no commanders or officers, because all are equal in Christ, therefore no masters nor officers, no laws nor orders, nor corrections nor punishments;—I say, I never denied, but in such

cases, whatever is pretended, the commander or commanders
may judge, resist, compel and punish such transgressors, according
to their deserts and merits.[37]

The letter had the desired effect; agitation against bearing arms
gradually ceased.

A second situation involving hostility to constituted law and
order took place in Williams' closing months in office. Several
members of the Quaker faith, who had begun arriving in Rhode
Island in 1656 to escape persecution in the Bay, voiced contempt
for civil authority and were called into court, where the case
against them was dismissed. That they could be hailed before the
law for their conduct evidently surprised the Quakers; there were
no future outbursts on their part against constituted authority.

In 1657, a third and far more serious predicament involved William Harris, whose uncontrolled personality had led him to write
a book denying the authority of civil government with the cry of
"No Lords, No Masters." Harris' interpretation of the Scriptures,
on which his ideas of anarchy were based, were deemed by the
commissioners trying him as having forced the Bible to maintain
"that he that can say it is his conscience ought not to yield subjection to any human order amongst men." While the case against
him was never resolved, the trial had a temporary beneficial result. Soon after it was held, Harris turned from his anarchic principles to the practice of law. In the numerous lawsuits he was
involved in for the next twenty years, all because of his desire to
obtain more land for himself and his heirs, Harris proved he was
infinitely gifted in finding ways to harass both Williams and the
rest of the Rhode Island settlers.

Because of these and similar actions against leaders of troublesome cliques and lesser culprits, Williams managed to make the
central government of the colony dominant over those of the
towns. So successful was he in working for unity amidst diversity
that Coddington fell into line in 1656, promising to submit "to the
authoritie . . . in the Colonie as it is now united. . . ."[38] Even
the Arnolds in Pawtuxet broke away from their dependence on
Massachusetts and obeyed the laws of Rhode Island. And Harris,
who remained a thorn in the flesh of his fellow settlers all his life,
was at least to be so under cover of the law.

## III   *Williams' Last Years, 1657–1683*

Williams retired from the presidency of Rhode Island in 1657, when the works for which he has justly become renowned had been completed. Yet in the quarter of century left him to live, he continued to serve his townspeople in various capacities despite the infirmities brought on "by age, lameness, and many other weaknesses." Among the offices he filled were those of commissioner, assistant deputy, clerk, and councilman. A letter written to John Winthrop, Jr., the son of his former friend, and now Governor of Connecticut, explained how the charter of 1663 granted Rhode Island by Charles II had brought him back to serve as assistant in the newly elected government of the colony; the letter also revealed the unselfishness of the man in always having worked for the public good as against any private gain: "I have since been occasioned and drawn (being nominated in the Charter to appear again upon the deck) from my beloved privacy; my humble desires are to contribute my poor mite (as I have ever, and I hope ever shall) to preserve plantation and public interest of the whole New England and not interest of this or that town, colony, opinion." [39]

Despite the royal charter of 1663, which set the eastern boundary line between Connecticut and Rhode Island at the Narragansett River, both colonies kept haggling over boundary lines for the next sixty years. If encroachments on Rhode Island from members of the New England Confederation who were determined to either dismember or swallow up the tiny colony were not enough, there was William Harris from within to contend with. In 1658, he began a series of lawsuits to obtain more land, which kept Rhode Islanders in an unsettled state of mind for almost a generation.

Aside from the Rhode Islanders' fierce love of independence and their reluctance to give up an untrammeled sense of individuality, the chief deterrent to a more unified colony during these years was the insatiable grabbing of unoccupied areas of southern Rhode Island territory by the leaders of the New England Confederation. In 1670, writing to Major Mason,[40] an old friend of the Pequot War days, Williams gave his views about this inordinate

greed for land. With his own values derived from a wholly different realm, the quest for "great portions of land, land in this
wilderness" he viewed as "a depraved appetite after the great
vanities, dreams and shadows of this vanishing life." Like a true
Puritan in his belief in damnation, he foresaw the consequences of
this greed as "one of the gods of New England, which the living
and most high Eternal will destroy and famish."

One notable event of these last years was his decision in 1672 to
dispute the tenets of Quakerism with the leader of the faith,
George Fox. While Fox never became his opponent, Williams
managed to engage three other Quakers in a debate which tar-
nished to some extent his reputation as an upholder of religious
freedom. As for his own religious affiliation, except for a short
period in 1639 when he held to the Baptist faith, Williams never
allied himself with any church after his separation from the Salem
congregation. Instead he became a Seeker, searching for a church
dispensation similar to that which obtained in the days of the
apostles. According to Callender, throughout his colonial life, Williams' religious fervor remained unquenched; and in his home-
town he "used to uphold a public worship" and for a number of
years held monthly services in the Narragansett country.[41]

The last public event of importance with which he was associated was King Philip's war in 1675. Prior to its outbreak, his services were called upon for the last time to negotiate with the Narragansetts; this time he failed to avert major hostilities, hostilities
no one could have averted because of the land defraudations
practiced for more than a half century against the Indians by
greedy speculators of the New England Confederation. Unsuc-
cessful, too, was his warning to the Quaker administration in
Providence to fortify the town. As a result, once the war was over,
the Narragansetts were crushed forever as a future threat to the
settlers, but not before the members of the Confederation suffered
heavy losses of life. Providence alone had more than one hundred
of its original one hundred and twenty-three houses destroyed.

Because of increasingly poor health and lameness during the
last seven years of his life, Williams largely withdrew from public
affairs. The exact date of his death like that of his birth, is unknown. From the available evidence, he died in 1683 sometime
between January 16 and March 15.[42] Short as history measures

time were his eighty years of life; still his unquenchable love of religious liberty for all will go down through the ages as a beacon light for future generations to follow in their quest to worship according to their conscience.

## CHAPTER 3

# The Bloudy Tenent and Related Works, 1643–1645

EXCEPT for *George Fox Digg'd Out of His Burrowes,* Williams' diatribe against the Quakers, all of his works, whether written in old or New England, were first published in the mother country. The first such occasion for publication came in the years 1643–45, when he was sent abroad by his fellow colonists to act as their agent in obtaining a charter for Rhode Island. Once arrived in his native land in the summer of 1643, Williams found the times unfavorable to press for his objective, since the Civil War had broken out the previous year. With Parliament, which was composed mainly of Puritans of the Presbyterian stripe, having grasped the reins of government left vacant by Charles's flight, and fearful of a royalist attack on London where parliamentary strength was centered, more important matters concerned them than a request for a patent for a small patch of land around Narragansett Bay.

Consequently, Williams bided his time, becoming acquainted with the current political and religious scene, as a result of which he was soon to start writing some of the tracts for which he is best known. He also took time to catch up with family affairs, visiting his brother Sydrach, with whom he united in instituting a suit at chancery against their youngest brother Robert, who, as executor of their mother's will, had failed to pay his two older brothers the legacies bequeathed them. The suit at law was lost, and years later Williams told the Quakers how his refusal to take an oath, an action they also objected to, cost him "the loss of great Sums." [1]

Some other people Williams managed to see during this period included Sir William Masham and Sir Thomas Barrington, both of whom he had served during his chaplaincy at Otes. As members of Parliament, both Masham and Barrington proved instrumental several months later in winning over to the side of those who were inclined to grant Williams his charter, the Earl of Warwick, the governor-in-chief of the English plantations.

## I    Key into the Language of America

On September 7, Williams managed to put through the press a *Key into the Language of America*,[2] a slim volume which outlined the culture of the Narragansetts in their own dialect. Containing some twenty-five hundred separate words, phrases, and sentences, the *Key* may be considered a definitive sociological text of early New England Indian life and mores, so completely had its author recorded the civilization of the tawny aborigines.

To understand why the *Key* came to be written, one must appreciate the motives behind the Puritan emigration to the new world. Escape from the persecution of Laud and Charles was a foremost cause, to be sure, but so, too, was the idea of converting the Indians. The original charter of the Massachusetts Bay Colony had in fact stated that "the propagation of the Gospel is the thing we do profess above all to be our aim in settling this Plantation." Yet, once settled in and around Boston in 1630, the Bay colonists became too busy cozening the natives out of their lands to give much thought to their lofty ideal.[3] Almost alone of the early settlers, Williams never appeared to have lost sight of the objective that had brought him to New England: his "longing after the natives' soules."

*New England's Prospects*, published in 1634 by William Wood, reveals how Williams went about pursuing his purpose: "One of the English Preachers, in a speciall good intent of doing good to their soules, hath spent much time in attaining to their Language, wherein he is so good a proficient, and he can speake to their understanding, and they to his; much loving and respecting him for his love and counsell. It is hoped that he may be an instrument of good amongst them." [4] Years later Williams corroborated Wood's observation that, from the very beginning, his "soul's desire was to do the natives good and to that end to have their language." [5] To that end, once in Plymouth, and later at Salem, Williams lodged in both the Wampanoags' and the Narragansetts' "filthy smoky holes . . . to gain their tongue." Other tribes whom he got to know through his trading, his peace-negotiating, and his

conversion activities included the Shawomets, Cowesetts, Nip-
mucs, Nyantics, Pequots, and the Mohawks.

Learning the Narragansett tongue could not have been difficult
for one who was already adept in Latin, Greek, and Hebrew, and
who throughout his life showed a remarkable flair for languages.
Since Christianization of the natives was his paramount objective,
learning the Narragansett and related Indian dialects must have
been regarded as a necessary first step, just as sleeping in their
wigwams and sharing their scanty repasts were but other ways of
getting an insight into their culture. That his efforts at conversion
slackened somewhat after his exile from the Bay cannot be
doubted. Having tasted the mercy dispensed by his Christian
brethren in banishing him, Williams may have become less than
enthusiastic about teaching and preaching a mode of life that his
own people failed to follow.

Nevertheless, the many notes he had taken on Indian life during his dozen years among them were brought together during his
first trip abroad, the few months at sea furnishing him the first
period of sustained leisure in more than ten years. The prefatory
letter to his "Deare and Welbeloved Friends and Counreymen, in
old and new England," revealed how and why he wrote his work:
"I drew the materialls in a rude lumpe at Sea, as a private helpe to
my own memory, that I might not by my present absence, lightly
lose what I had so dearely bought in some few yeares hardships,
and charges among the Barbarians; yet being reminded by some,
what pitie it were to bury those Materialls in my Grave at land or
Sea, and withall, remembring how oft I have been importun'd by
worthy friends of all sorts, to afford them some helps this way." [6]

As a result, he hoped the "Key" to "the Native Language"
would "unlock some Rarities concerning the Natives themselves,
not yet discovered." In thus giving his native countrymen an in-
sider's view of the Indians and their civilization, the work was
automatically assured of success. For from the time Indians first
began to appear in England as captives, where they were shown
in public places in London, the English were not only hungry for
information about the aborigines of the New World, but were
also seriously concerned about their Christianization. Especially
after Massachusetts Bay became established, practical results
along these lines were eagerly awaited. Williams himself noted

that the question at issue was the diligence with which the colonists went about the task of converting the natives.[7]

According to Robert Baillie, who was to become one of Williams' foremost opponents in the matter of religious freedom, the Rhode Islander was practically alone in his concern for the natives. Criticizing the Bay Puritans, who, he felt, neglected their missionary opportunities, Baillie went on to remark: "I have read of none of them that seem to have minded this matter: onely Williams in the time of his banishment from among them did assay what could be done with those desolate souls, and by a little experience quickly did find a wonderful great facility to gain thousands of them. . . ."[8]

A former resident of the Bay, Thomas Lechford, writing in 1642, told how the ministers there had tried the unusual expedient of preaching the gospel to the natives in English. When no conversions resulted, the clerics were not at all nonplussed. "Unlesse they come to heare and learn English," the Indians would have only themselves to blame in failing to be Christianized.[9] The only exception among them apparently was John Eliot, the famous apostle to the Massachusetts Indians, who made the New Testament available to them in 1661 in their own dialect.

Yet, however much Williams may have been concerned with the natives' souls, his *Key* was no tract for conversion. Divided into thirty-two chapters, the work dealt, as part of the title indicated, with the "Customes, Manners and worships, of the Aforesaid natives, in Peace and Warre, in Life and Death." For this purpose Williams had "rune through varieties of Intercourses with them Day and Night, Summer and Winter, by Land and Sea."[10]

The chapter headings alone denote the thoroughness with which he went about the business of setting down what he knew of Indian customs and habits. Once past the data on salutations, the reader is introduced to such aspects of native life as their foodstuffs and entertainment, their habits of sleep, their houses and family relationships, and the names for the various parts of the body. Then follow such topics as nature, the heavenly bodies, the great outdoors, and animal life, all of which give rise to sections on travel, the seasons of the year, the weather and winds, the earth and its produce, and the various kinds of beasts to be found in New England. Outdoor occupations like hunting and fishing are discussed as well as business matters like trading and money. Likewise treated are public affairs, like government and war, and private ones such as marriage, sickness, and love of news and discourse. The religion of the Indians, as one would expect, constitutes the longest chapter in the work.

How direct and useful were the exchanges in the "implicite Dialogue," the form Williams had settled on, can be seen by studying a few of them. Thus, on the matter of war, we read the following: "I am angry. Why are you angry? He struck me. You are a quarreller." The subject of news and discourse evokes these ideas: "Who brought this news? Of whom did you hear it? Your news is true. I cannot speak your language." The institution of marriage brings forth the following: "He goes a wooing. He is my son-in-law. He hath wronged my bed."

Aside from its value for anyone wishing to know what the language and habits of the Narragansetts were before these were modified by their association with the English, the *Key* is also important for the light it sheds on an unexpected facet of Williams' character. In its pages is revealed a colonist deeply interested in the New World and its natives, a milieu far different from the religious and political one into which he was shortly to plunge himself. When environed by the natives, Williams' mind was free to make observations when a phrase or sentence that he had listed set off a definite train of thought. Thus, "their pounding Morter," in his chapter on family relationships, has this comment following it: "Their women constantly beat all their corne with hand: they plant it, dresse it, gather it, barne it, beat it, and take as much paines as any people in the world, which labour is questionlesse one cause of the extraordinary ease of childbirth"(65).

In speaking of fruits, he has this to say of the strawberry: "This Berry is the wonder of all the Fruits growing naturally in those parts: It is of it selfe Excellent; so that one of the chiefest Doctors of England was wont to say, that God could have made, but God never did make a better Berry. . . ." (121).

Here one almost senses the enjoyment Williams experienced as he contemplated with pleasure and interest the many different facets of the new civilization to which his savage companions had introduced him. Still the man was not merely an observer; he was also an able minister. Hence the "particular" observations, which he set down in quotations, at the end of each section, were his attempts to correlate what he had seen with some higher meaning. So the sea, where the larger fish are constantly devouring the smaller ones, became, metaphorically, an area where Christians were persecuted.

> Christ's little ones must hunted be
> Devour'd; yet rise as Hee.
> And eate up those which now awhile
> Their fierce devourers be. (142)

Again, the nakedness of the Indians gave rise to the spiritual covering worn by Christians.

> Israell was naked, wearing cloathes!
> The best clad English-man,
> Not cloth'd with Christ, more naked is:
> Than naked Indian. (146)

In many of his observations the practices of the English came off second best in comparison with those of the Indians. Unwilling to write them off as mere heathens, as the Bay had done, Williams found much that was praiseworthy in the redskins, who had incidentally become that color "by the Sunne and their annoyntings," but who were actually "borne white" (80). Early in his acquaintance with them he had been favorably impressed with their civility, courtesy, and moral nature, and of the last trait had written that he "could never discerne that excesse of scandalous sins amongst them, which Europe aboundeth with. Drunkenness and gluttony, generally they know not what sinnes they be; . . . [neither does] a man . . . heare of such crimes amongst them of robberies, murthers, adulteries, as amongst the English" (165). Later, when he got to know them better, he changed his mind, noting their drunkenness, "lying, stealing, whoring, murdering" (165).

But, before their immoral and licentious qualities became apparent and before he became doubtful about transmitting the benefits of Christianity to them, Williams had spent much time preaching the gospel to the Narragansetts. At his first coming, as in most primitive societies, he found a polytheistic people who branched "their God-head into thirty seven Gods" to cover the

many phases of nature that they believed intervened in their lives
(16). In two cardinal points, though, their beliefs coincided with
Christian dogma: that God existed and that He rewarded those
who diligently sought Him. From this premise they attributed all
excellence to Deity and designated success in hunting as a mark of
His favor; conversely, loss of children and accidents were regarded as signs of His anger and displeasure.

Since none of Williams' sermons to the natives have survived,
his own narration of an incident will have to serve as an indication
of what must have been his spellbinding magnetism as a preacher.
Finding himself once in the midst of a tribe with whose dialect he
was unacquainted, and therefore unable to "speak to them to their
understandings," he yet held forth so persuasively "of the True
and living and only Wise God . . . that at parting many burst
forth Oh when will you come againe, to bring us some more
newes of this God?" (49). In general, he found the savages concerned about their spiritual state and envious of the English for
their Bible, which the Indians felt had more to say about the soul's
eventual destination than they, who possessed no "books and writings" on the subject. In speaking to them about "the rising againe
of the body," Williams found one who "cryed out, I shall never
believe this" (84).

That some failed to absorb the idea of resurrection did not
trouble Williams, for such was the esteem in which the Narragansetts normally held him that many would readily have converted
to Christianity, had he so desired it. This failure to convert them
however, was later held against him. For paradoxically enough,
once the *Key* was published and Williams' activities in behalf of
the Indians noted, the Bay Puritans were shamed into active
missionary work. Publishing false figures testifying to the great
success of their efforts, the Bay historians downgraded their foe
who had no such report to make. Williams—commenting on the
influence he wielded over Canonicus and his people, who were
thinking of "keeping the Englishmans day of worship," a practice
he "could easily have brought the Countrey to"—was far too
honest to believe that the soul of the average Indian was ready for
a true Christianity. His reason was simple: "I was persuaded, and
am, that Gods way is first to turne from it's Idolls, both of heart,
worship, and conversation, before it is capable of worship, to the
true and living God" (160–61).

The absence of a true repentance on the part of the natives was one thing; unfortunately, the lack of a similar sense of contrition was also "the bane of million of soules in England, and all other Nations professing to be Christian Nations who are brought by publique authority of Baptisme and fellowship with God in Ordinances of worship, before the saving worke of Repentance, and a true turning to God" (161). No doubt this failure among "Christian Nations" to follow the normal process of repentance in becoming truly religious also cooled his original ardor to convert the redskins. Yet in *Christenings Make Not Christians,* a later tract he wrote on the subject of conversion, Williams added other reasons that made understandable his refusal to employ his talents in this area of the ministry.

Had it not been for the publication of the *Key,* it is doubtful whether Williams would have obtained his charter. For among the many Englishmen vitally interested in Indian life were the eighteen commissioners of colonial plantations; and one of these was Sir Henry Vane, the same Vane with whom Williams had become so friendly in the Bay just before he was banished, and with whom he had shared similar beliefs in regard to absolute religious freedom. Vane had come a long way in the eight years since he, an unreliable but winsome young man of twenty-two, had first arrived in and later left Massachusetts. To honor him and his famous father, in 1636 the Bay officials had appointed the younger Vane governor of their colony. But his abhorrence of compulsory and uniform worship was intensified by what he saw in Massachusetts, and he was more than ever convinced of the need for seekers of the light to go their own respective ways in matters of faith. By 1643, he had grown sufficiently to become perhaps the ablest administrator of the Puritan Revolution.

On March 14, 1644, thanks to Vane's efforts in winning over the required number of commissioners, Williams was granted his charter. At the same time, however, certain forces were at work which might have nullified Vane's efforts in his friend's behalf. One such deterrent was the Bay, who since 1641, had been trying to obtain a patent which would have placed the Narragansett Bay area under her jurisdiction. As a colony standing for orthodoxy, and with Williams' colony all but unknown, the Bay stood a good chance of obtaining her objective. In fact, Thomas Weld, her agent in London, managed to procure a document that passed as a Narragansett patent; but this document later proved to be fraudulent.[11] Against these machinations of the Bay, Williams' quest, without Vane's help, might have gone for naught, since Weld was as highly skilled a negotiator as himself in dickering with the commissioners.

The *Key*, with its account of what Williams had already done for the Indians, was, despite Vane's aid, a determining factor in winning him his patent, a probability reinforced by the letter given him and signed by various members of the Parliament. To be handed the Bay upon his return to New England in 1644, the letter was intended to effect a rapprochement between the Rhode Islander and the oligarchy; and, among other informative items, it referred to Williams' "great industry and travail in his printed Indian labours." [12]

## II  Mr. Cotton's Letter Examined and Answered

One reason why Williams had difficulty in having his request for a charter even considered during the summer of 1643 was that the Civil War was going badly for the Puritans. As yet Cromwell's Ironsides were still in training and would not for some time take the field against the Royalists, whom they eventually vanquished. But in mid-1643, to prevent a possible encirclement of London by Charles's forces, Parliament sought help from Scotland and sent Vane to Edinburgh in early August to accept the Solemn League and Covenant, the only terms on which the Scots would proffer aid. Sworn to by Parliament on September 25, the Covenant committed England to a qualified Presbyterianism similar to that which obtained in Scotland. The imposition of a presbytery to replace Laud's episcopacy, which had been overthrown following the flight of Charles, was distasteful to many liberal Puritans, who like Milton, would soon begin to think of the new Scottish presbyter as nothing more than the old Anglican priest writ large. Still there was no alternative if twenty thousand Scottish troops were to be made available to fight against Charles. To soften the impact of the new religion, Vane had included in the Covenant the phrase "according to the word of God," a reservation which allowed, for purposes of debate, the use of certain scriptural practices in worship as against those employed by the Presbyterians.

As if to implement the purpose of the Covenant, the Westmin-

ster Assembly, called into being on June 12, 1643, had been ordered by Parliament to draw up a model of church government
for the country. Having had its origin in a request by disaffected
Puritans for a synod which Charles had refused to call, the Assembly had joined Parliament in swearing to uphold the Covenant.
Comprised mostly of eminent clergymen from both Scotland and
England, most of whom were Presbyterians, and of a small minority of Independents, the Assembly led by its intolerant majority of
Presbyterians was prepared in the fall of 1643 to institute a strict
national church, one similar to Scotland's, in which there would
be little or no toleration for Nonconformists.

Outnumbered as they were, the more liberal Independents, led
by Vane and Cromwell, sought ways both in Parliament and in
the Assembly, to keep the Presbyterians from stifling dissenters
altogether. For this purpose and in order to overcome the Presbyterian majority, they began to woo the many sects then current,
almost all of whom were inclined toward Separatism. At this juncture, to counteract the charge of Separatism which was leveled
against them, five conservative Independent ministers in their
*Apologeticall Narration,* which appeared in January, 1644, claimed
they sought instead a middle way "betwixt that which is falsely
charged upon us, Brownisme; and that which is the contention of
these times, the authoritative Presbyteriall Government. . . ." [13]
But their idea of "a middle way" was a church form of government in which Congregationalism rather than Presbyterianism
best served the needs of the nation. And for their model they held
up the New England brand of Congregationalism fostered by
John Cotton, in which no toleration was allowed.

Of these developments toward the establishment of a new
church polity, Williams kept posted. Busy as he was with family
affairs, with publishing the *Key,* and working indefatigably for his
charter, Williams still found time to attend many of the stormy
sessions of the Westminster Assembly. There, according to Baillie, one of the Scotch divines deeply committed to the idea of
setting up an English church similar to Scotland's, Williams was
so persuasive with both ministers and laymen alike that he drew
"a great number after him to a singular Independencie." [14]

The anomalous and compromising position of the Independents
—who hobnobbed with the toleration-minded sects but simultaneously lauded Cotton as the exponent of the New England Way

—was all that was needed to launch Williams in his role of polem-
icist. To help him in his new role was a letter Cotton had written
him shortly after his flight from Salem; this he had taken to England, together with other communications he meant to use as occasion gave rise. Cotton had originally penned his letter in order
to absolve himself from the charge of having influenced the magistrates' verdict, which in any event he felt "to be righteous in the
eyes of God." Seven years later, after he had probably forgotten
all about the matter, Cotton was to rue the fact he had ever expressed his approval. For on February 5, 1644, just a few months
after the *Key* had been published and copies of *A Letter of Mr.
John Cotton to Mr. Williams* had somehow mysteriously appeared
on London bookstalls, Williams published *Mr. Cotton's Letter
Examined and Answered,* in which he gave his own account of
the events leading to his exile.[15] In one fell swoop he was not only
to topple Cotton from the lofty perch where he had been placed
by the Independent ministers by revealing him as a persecutor; he
was also to expose the lack of logic inherent in the position of the
Nonseparatists. A more propitious time for Williams' answer to
appear could not have been chosen, what with his own name
fresh in the public's mind because of the popularity of the *Key.*
Cotton, always newsworthy, was especially so now because of the
appearance of his old letter to Williams.

In the main, *Mr. Cotton's Letter Examined and Answered* is
Williams' version of the events leading to his banishment as well
as a defense of his Separatist position. An explanatory note "to the
Impartiall Reader" made him immediately aware of the severe
hardships Williams had suffered because of his expulsion. Held
accountable for these hardships was Cotton, who countercharged
that "had you perished, your blood had beene on your owne head;
it was your sinne to procure it, and your sorrow to suffer it." [16]
After that harsh judgment, Williams had stopped writing to his
adversary; and, while disclaiming any responsibility for the present appearance of Cotton's letter on the London bookstalls, he
rejoiced that providence had given him "present opportunity of
Answer."

For Williams there were many things for Cotton to answer, as,
for example, the latter's having addressed him on the one hand, as
one "Beloved in Christ," and this beloved one soon finding himself "for no other cause, then shall presently appeare be denyed

the common aire to breathe in and a civill cohabitation upon the same earth." [17] And, if this harsh treatment was all that could be expected while Cotton himself was professedly seeking more light, the question was posed—what kind of treatment could Christ Jesus expect if he "[or] any of his servants shall be pleased to hold forth a further light" than that entertained by Cotton? [18]

This gap between Cotton's intentions (professing to seek more light) and his actual performance (persecution) revealed the difference between the Bay's thinking and Williams' on the role of the Bible and its applicability to current affairs. Since his early conversion to Puritanism, Williams' desire to know God's will had been an ever growing one, and an unceasing study of the Scriptures had become a means to that end. Believing as he did that no one was ever too old to grow in grace and that Christ Jesus had commanded his followers "to try all things," [19] Williams' entire approach to the concept of progress and revelation was an open-ended and progressive one, in which the accession of new light swept away the errors that lesser illumination had previously been responsible for. This outlook was diametrically opposed to the Bay's static concept in which God had revealed himself once and for all in the Bible, with no further revelations ever to be expected. As Perry Miller has so aptly stated the matter in his text on *The Puritans*, "Puritan history was posited upon the assumption of an eternal sameness in things, their perpetual control by the same agency for the same ends." Yet Williams was certain that, were the Bay elect to leave themselves open for more light, they would cease persecuting those who did not differ with them in essential dogma, "but only in the way and manner of the administrations of Jesus Christ." [20]

To bolster his case that Williams had been completely responsible for his banishment, Cotton had charged his adversary with various derelictions; one was Williams' having forsaken his church at Salem and thus having cut his congregation off from its necessary "spirituall corn." This offense Williams minimized and likened it to Jesus' command forbidding his apostles "to preach at all to some places, at some times." Another of Cotton's accusations centered on "the sandiness of those grounds" or the basic premises of Williams' reasoning, which had led eventually to his exile. In turn, Cotton was reminded that, since his own removal to New England, he had come around to confess "the sandiness of the grounds" of certain practices he had engaged in while residing in the mother country. What was more, he had even come to view the objections Williams had made against the Book of Common Prayer as "rockie" or sound.[21]

Cotton had referred to the sentence passed upon the Salem minister as a banishment from the churches; this left him open to Williams' indictment that the relationship between state and church in the Bay was similar to the connection between the Anglican Church and the Stuarts, a union the Puritans had protested against in the mother country. Else why had Cotton referred to the sentence imposed upon Williams as "a banishment from the Churches, except he silently confesse, that the frame or constitution of their Churches is but implicitly National which yet they professe against for otherwise was I not permitted to live in the world, or Commonweale, except for this reason, that the Common-weale and Church is yet but one, and hee that is banished from the one must necessarily bee banished from the other also" (326–27). Another example Williams offered of Bay intolerance involved a number of English Presbyterians who were forbidden from emigrating to the Bay, where they had hoped to engage in their own mode of worship. Although accounted "eminent for personall godlinesse," these would-be emigrants were informed not to depart for New England unless they meant to conform to the Congregationalist mode of worship (349).

In his overwhelming desire to make Williams completely responsible for his banishment, Cotton finally admitted that the court may have sentenced Williams not so much for having neglected his Salem congregation as, "for ought I know, for your corrupt Doctrines [Separatism], which tend to the disturbance both of civil and holy peace" (334). "The disturbance of both civill and holy peace" was all Williams needed to set forth for the first time the essentially different and distinct offices of church and state and to indicate how careful he was that none of his doctrines tend "to the breach of holy or civill peace, of which I have ever desired to be unfainedly tender, acknowledging the Ordinance of Magistracie to be properly, and adequately fitted by God, to preserve the civill State in civill peace and order." God had also "appointed a spirituall Government and Governours in matters pertaining to his worship and the consciences of men, both which Governments, Governours, Laws, Offences, Punishments, are Essentially distinct, and the confounding of them brings all the world into Combustion" (335).

Cotton's charge that Williams should have appreciated being expelled from a commonwealth where he "could not enjoy holy fellowship with any Church of God amongst them without sin," again furnished Williams with the opportunity to show the dissimilar offices of church and state. Citing Cotton's claim as a dangerous one, since history could furnish examples of famous states "wherein [was] known no Church of Jesus Christ," Cotton was also reminded of his intended desire only a few years previously to throw in his lot with Anne Hutchinson and the rest of the Antinomians. His doing so would, of course, have meant "dissent from the New England Churches," an action which Cotton "was upon the point to doe in a separation from the Churches there as legall" (337). This reminder hit home since the English Independents realized how close to heresy the great examplar of the New England Way had come in 1637 because of his early attachment to the Antinomians.

Like all good Puritans who saw in every aspect of life a manifestation of God's will, Cotton viewed the serious illness Williams suffered shortly after his sentence as an expression of God's justice upon his foe. Williams in turn was content to have God judge which of the two was serving him better, he or Cotton, whom he termed "swimming with the stream of outward credit and profit, and smiting with the fist and sword of persecution such as dare not joyn in worship with him" (339).

What becomes apparent amidst all the charges and countercharges between the two ministers is that in their respective stands as a Separatist or Nonseparatist, their views clashed on what constituted the "true" church. In admonishing Cotton who claimed to see and practice what "so many thousands of godly persons of higher note in all ages since the Apostacie saw not," Williams bade his correspondent consider carefully the following: "First, concerning the nature of a particular Church, to consist only of holy and godly persons. Secondly, of a true Ministrie called by that Church. Thirdly, a true Worship free from Ceremonies, Common-Prayer. Fourthly, a true Government in the hands only of such Governours and Elders, as are appointed by the Lord Jesus" (347).

The saintliness of the persons constituting the particular

churches was of major concern to Williams, who, like Cotton, believed a true church should consist solely of godly people. But over the degree of godliness that church members manifested the two men differed. True, the Nonseparatists sought as members for their congregations only those in whom they discerned "true Regeneration," but at the same time Cotton did not think it necessary for these applicants to "bewaile all the Pollutions which they have been defiled within the former Church-fellowship." But on this last point Williams was more than insistent. Those seeking church membership needed not only to remove themselves from "former pollutions," but they also required "a second kind of Regeneration" in which they became convinced "of the evill of the false Church, Ministry, Worship" (350). It was lack of foresight that had made them unaware of the "the evill of a Nationall Church"; once aware of this evil, however, "there necessarily follows a withdrawing from the Church, Ministry and Worship of the false Christ, and submission unto the true" (368).

Until this step was taken, the Bay Congregationalists were simply not holy enough for Williams. Therefore, Cotton's hostility toward Separatism and his allegiance to the Church of England, or his "walke in the midst of 2 extremes," Williams found completely illogical and inadmissable; this was especially so in light of Cotton's threefold admission "that no Nationall, Provinciall, Diocesan, or Parish Church are true Churches"; that "a Church of Christ cannot be constituted of such godly persons who are in bondage to the inordinate love of the world"; and that "if a Church consist of such, God's people ought to be separate from them" (375–76). Then why, Williams queried, did not Cotton separate from the parish churches of England, which were filled with "unregenerate persons, and of thousands inbondaged" to the worst forms of fleshly sin (376)? To Cotton's rebuttal that God "had not prospered the way of Separation," Williams could only reply that in the past even true churches had suffered a lack of peace; and the chief reason false churches currently enjoyed a sense of quiet was that their members feared to rebel and suffer civil punishment (383).

Still if disengagement from the Church of England was the first step to insure a true church and a pure worship, Williams was no less adamant about what constituted "a true Ministerie," and here he clarified his difference of opinion with those New England

Congregationalists, who on visits to the mother country, attended Anglican services. For him there were two different offices to the ministry, one of which was constituted of "the ordinarie Ministers of the Gospel [who] are Pastors, Teachers, Bishops, Overseers, Elders, and . . . their proper worke is to feed and govern a truly converted, holy and godly people, gathered into a flock or Church estate, and not properly preachers to convert, beget, make Disciples, which the Apostles and Evangelists professedly were (386).

It was, therefore, a dangerous disorder when these two different aspects of the ministry were not kept distinct and "many excellent and worthy persons mainly preach for conversion, as conceiving and that truly the body of the people of England to be in a naturall and unregenerate estate: and yet account they themselves fixed and constant Officers and Ministers to particular Parishes or congregations, unto whom they also administer the holy things of God" (388).

No less important that the above two distinctions of the ministerial office was the "lawful calling . . . according to Christ Jesus" of those who entered the ministry. Cotton was reminded that upon his arrival in New England, despite his previous ministry in the mother country, he had merely considered himself a "private Christian" until he had received "a calling from a particular Church." But now that he was firmly in the saddle in Boston, the word had been laid down "that Christ Jesus hath appointed no other calling to the Ministrie, but such as they practice in New England" (390). All others who did not preach in a particular Congregational church were regarded as "none of Christs."

As has been indicated in the *Key*, one reason Williams did not give himself wholeheartedly to the conversion of the Narragansetts was his doubt that he had been called to this work "according to Christ Jesus." On his second trip abroad in 1651, his doubt that ministers who were employed and paid by the state were called of Christ led to his writing *The Hireling Ministry None of Christs*, in which he elaborated more fully on this matter of calling. For the time he was content to know, that the ministry and church he had in mind could be constantly sought after, despite the civil and spiritual disturbances brought on by the Civil War.

In a passionate peroration charging Cotton with actually enjoying and practicing separation while withholding the same privilege from others, Williams lashed his persecutor with this query: "If the Lord Jesus were himselfe in person in Old or New England, what Church, what Ministry, what Worship, what Government he would set up, and what persecution he would practice toward them that would not receive Him?" (396).

There Williams let the matter drop. The question itself disclosed the premise on which his thinking was posited. Those who professed to be followers of Christ Jesus and still persecuted others on matters of conscience were given something to think about. In future tracts he would make clear that it was a church after the pattern set forth by the master Christian and the Apostles that he was intent upon re-establishing, since its original succession had broken down with the Apostasy. Following the publication of *Mr. Cotton's Letter Examined and Answered*, Cotton's prestige as the exponent of the New England Way was severely damaged. The English Independents were also badly hurt and lost the numerical help of the sectaries, once the latter realized the intolerance and bigotry they could expect from the Independents, English or New English style.

### III  Queries of Highest Consideration

Viewed in proper perspective *Mr. Cotton's Letter Examined and Answered* can be regarded as the first salvo of a triple-mounted attack of the persecuting policies practiced by Cotton and the New England orthodoxy. The second work in this barrage was *Queries of Highest Consideration*,[22] which was rushed into print on February 9, 1644, just four days after *Mr. Cotton's Letter Examined and Answered*. Where the latter tract was written to reveal the casuistry inherent in the idea of Nonseparation, *Queries*, which was addressed to the Westminster Assembly, was penned to discuss and disprove the ideas set forth in the *Apologeticall Narration*, which had appeared early in January. In their attempt in this work to advance Congregationalism as the only true church policy for England, Messrs. Goodwin, Bridge, Burroughs, Simpson, and Nye, the five Independent ministers concerned, had proclaimed their position as the middle way between Separatism and its extremism on the one hand, and Presbyterianism and its authoritarianism on the other.

But behind this assertion Williams saw the same manifestations of illiberality and intolerance that underlay its New England counterpart, in which the close relationship between church and state had resulted in a rigid orthodoxy from which dissenters were banished. In the five dissenting brethren's statement that they did not wish to remove from the Church of England but merely to purify it, Williams heard again the same arguments previously employed by the Bay brethren before they had migrated to Massachusetts, but who for all practical purposes practiced separation from the Anglican Church. Had Williams had the slightest doubt which road English Independency meant to take, as it was outlined in the *Apologeticall Narration,* it was completely dispelled by *A Model of Church and Civil Power,* one of a number of documents he had taken with him to England, and which gave the Bay position on the right of magistrates to intervene in church affairs.

Williams obtained a copy of the *Model* after he had fled from Salem, and a reading of it only confirmed for him that the church-state relationship that the Bay Independents had worked out for themselves by 1635 was exactly what the English Independents in 1644 were attempting to establish in the mother country. Again, with the many sects concerned about religious persecution and how far the Presbyterians in the assembly would insist upon conformity, Williams thought the time was ripe to show how the English Independents and Presbyterians were both wrong in seeking to found their own particular kind of state church and to enlist the aid of Parliament in so doing. For, if the legislators were to choose their country's church, the issue to Williams was clear: it did not matter which of the two groups won the right to impose its form of church government; in either case, the resulting national church would again be "forcing the consciences of all men to one Worship."

In his answer to Cotton, Williams had held forth solely to his adversary; in *Queries* he spoke to the entire English nation. For, in his desire to obtain as wide an audience as possible Williams not only had addressed the work to the two religious factions concerned, but had also worked in a few introductory remarks which he wished Parliament to consider—remarks Cotton later labeled as "high thoughts" in that he thought Williams was presumptuous in having addressed them to the governing body of the nation. But Williams was fighting for convictions for which he had already suffered, and he was not disposed to be timid even though he was addressing Parliament. In fact, he considered himself "humbly bold," as fine an oxymoron as he could have coined to describe the tone and tenor of his inquiries. Moreover, a more apt assessment of his character would be difficult to imagine. Humble he was in the sense that he was merely a single individual broaching his views; bold, in that he had something substantial to say and was going to say it.

Aware of the pressures being brought to bear upon the parliamentarians by the Westminster Assembly to institute Presbyterianism as the national religion,[23] and mindful of his own experience at the hands of the Bay magistrates, Williams warned the lawmakers of the turbulence and confusion that could be expected whenever civil authority intervened in church matters: "Your Wisdomes Know the Fatall Miscarriages of Englands Parliaments in this point; what setting up, pulling downe, what Formings, Reformings, and againe Deformings. . . ."[24] Still, if the lawmakers did not allow themselves to be completely swept away by the idea of a national church, Williams thought "some higher Act concerning Religion, attends and becomes your Consultations."

In the twelve queries Williams "propounded to the five . . . Ministers and the Scotch Commissioners" of the Assembly were to be found some of his more important ideas: his insistence that the civil magistrate had jurisdiction solely in the civil realm, and that Jesus was the model whereby Christians could gauge their own thoughts and actions, especially in the matter of persecution. Two other concepts included his conviction that all religious groups, including Catholics, were entitled to absolute freedom of conscience, and that Parliament possessed no more power than that bestowed upon it by the people.

Believing as he did that Jesus' example in church problems should serve as a precedent for the practices of latter-day Christians, Williams actually questioned the right of the Westminster divines to have convened in the first place, as there was no mandate for such a synod in any "Precept or Pattern" of Jesus. As for their endeavor to impose a uniform church on their countrymen, where in Christ's teaching was there any sanction for "a whole Nation or Kingdome to walk in one way of Religion?" (264) And what made either the Independent or the Presbyterian ministers so certain that a national church would accommodate everyone "without a racking and tormenting of the Soules as of the Bodies of persons," since it did not seem "possible to fit it to every conscience (265–66). To think otherwise would result in a "world of hypocrites."

Concerned as Williams was with the purest kind of Christianity, he admonished both factions that "living stones," or true believers, were needed as builders of the house of God; but this condition could come about only when souls were instilled with "the first principle of Christianity, Repentance." But since so few in England and Scotland, let alone the nobility and the gentry, were sincerely "regenerate and converted," it would be best to have these unregenerate ones become aware "how impossible it is for a dead Stone to have fellowship with the living God, and for any man to enter the Kingdome of God, without a second Birth" (261–262). Here Williams was concerned with a pure body of saints coming together in worship, as a result of true reformation, which for him meant a separation from the abominations that characterized the worship of a national church whether run by Independents or Presbyterians.

As for civil magistrates, their jurisdiction lay in the civil realm; in this area they had every right to "execute vengeance against Robbers, Murtherers, Tyrants." But, since the Independents and Presbyterians were intent upon having Parliament reform the English church—each in its own image—these officials who derived their power from the people were in effect having "the Nation, the Kingdome, and the whole world . . . rule and govern the Church," a state of affairs manifestly absurd (259).

Had not the confident boldness of Williams' ideas been enough at this point to incur the hostility of the hardbitten divines, who were intent only in ramming through their own brand of religious orthodoxy, his suggestion that Papists be allowed freedom of conscience would have done so. For Williams, it was all too obvious what would take place were any group of religionists deprived of their right to worship, and were church and state to become closely allied again in England: "For . . . if Englands Government were the Government of the whole World, not onley They, but a world of Idolaters of all sorts, yea the whole World must be driven out of the World" (267). Forward-looking as the idea was of granting Catholics freedom of worship, Williams badly misread the national mood at this particular juncture. Too little time had elapsed for Englishmen to forget the internecine warfare that had taken place between Protestants and Catholics prior to Elizabeth's ascension to the throne.

It was in the desire of both the Independents and the Presbyterians "to want more light" that Williams noted the contradiction between their respective intentions and performance. In view of their profession, how could they then in good conscience persecute other religionists "as Schismatiques, Hereticks, that believe they see a further Light and dare not joyn with either of your Churches?" (273). Striking hard at the Puritan bromide that God prospered only those lands that tolerated one faith, Williams observed that the Netherlands' stand as a haven for all kinds of dissenters had in no way been detrimental to her great prosperity. As for the Netherlands allowing the tares, or the sects, "to have a civill being in the field of the world," Williams believed it was necessary to seek the counsel of "the great and wisest Polititian that ever was, the Lord Jesus Christ" (274).

In a powerful conclusion Williams resorted to typology, an allegorical mode of interpreting the Bible, in which Hebrew history, fascinating as it might be as part of the Holy Scriptures, was invalid, superseded as it was by the advent of Christianity. Consequently, the Westminster divines were reminded of the persecutions that would follow should either a Presbyterian or Congregational church government be established, modeled as it would be after that of the Hebrews in which "the head of all is . . . Moses not Christ. . . ." In a mounting crescendo of phrases in which he released his overwhelming feelings on the difference between a government where church and state were separated, and one which was modeled after the Hebraic state, Williams indicated that, if the latter were instituted, it would be

Opposite to the very nature of a Christian Church, and the only holy Nation and Israel of God. Opposite to the very tender Bowels of Humanity, (how much more of Christianity?) . . . Opposite to the very Essentialls and Fundamentalls of the Nature of a Civill Magistracie, A Civil Commonweal or combination of Men, which can only respect civill things. . . . Opposite to the civill Peace, and the lives of Millions, slaughter'd upon this ground, in mutuall persecuting each others Conscience, especially the Protestant and the Papist. Opposite to the Souls of all Men, who by persecutions are ravished into a dissembled Worship, which their Hearts im-

brace not. Opposite to the best of Gods servants, who in all Popish
and Protestant States have been commonly esteemed and persecuted, as the only Schismaticks, Hereticks. Opposite to that
Light of Scripture which is expected yet to shine, which must by
that Doctrine be supprest as a new or old Heresie or Noveltie. All
this in all Ages experience testifies, which never saw any long
liv'd Fruit of Peace or Righteousnesse to grow upon that fatall
Tree. (275)

Had he attacked either the Presbyterians or the Independents
alone, Williams' diatribe would have been answered. But since
both were indicted, there was no response. Published anonymously, *Queries* was soon attributed to its author because of its
subject matter and style. In light of his stand against an established church in his rejoinder to Cotton, it became evident that no
one but Williams would have lashed out at both the Presbyterians
and the Independents in their attempt to impose religious conformity on an entire nation. With both his answer to Cotton's letter, and *Queries* having served as preliminaries, so to speak, to
whet his appetite for the battle of religious liberty and human
rights, Williams was now ready to make a major contribution to
this cause.

### IV   The Bloudy Tenent of Persecution

As forthright and direct as his indictment of both the Independent and Presbyterian divines of the Westminster Assembly
had been, Williams' real target in *Queries of Highest Consideration* was primarily Cotton and the Bay. This he made absolutely
clear in his most important work, *The Bloudy Tenent of Persecution*, the final blow of his threefold attack against the Massachusetts oligarchy. Appearing on July 15, 1644, when the pamphlet
war was at its height, with a spate of uncensored pamphlets being
written by authors who either defended or attacked the views of
the Independents and the Presbyterians, Williams' tract further
inflamed the already highly combustible feelings of the sectarians
who, concerned with religious toleration, were opposed to the
conformity desired by the two groups in the Assembly.

Williams' *Mr. Cotton's Letter Examined and Answered* had
been conceived as a rejoinder to the harsh sentence accorded him
by the Bay magistrates; *The Bloudy Tenent* had its inception as

the result of a reply Cotton had written in 1635 to some notes by an Anabaptist who had been sent to Newgate prison for his unorthodox beliefs. As in his original letter, justifying the magistrates' verdict against Williams, Cotton gave in his answer to the Anabaptist prisoner further evidence of his intolerance by insisting upon the validity of persecution for the cause of conscience. To refute Cotton's thesis, Williams hurriedly put together his major work which actually had its genesis in Providence. There he had received Cotton's response to the Anabaptist from one Master Hall of Roxbury, who, dissatisfied with the Boston minister's preemptory strictures on religious toleration, had sent the material to Williams for his opinion.

Simultaneous with his receipt of Cotton's reply, Williams had obtained a copy of *A Model of Church and Civil Power*, and he, who never forgot the harsh winter exile he had suffered because of his differences with the Bay, must have clung tenaciously to both. *The Bloudy Tenent* is indeed ample testimony of how well he turned these two papers to account. For his purpose, Williams divided the work into two halves, constituting in all one hundred and thirty-eight short chapters. The first part was a word-for-word rebuttal of Cotton's defense of persecution, with Williams' own fervent plea for liberty of conscience as a basic human right set forth in ringing phrases. The second half comprised his attack on the *Model*, in which he stressed the absolute necessity of separation of church and state, which, based on his concept of the civil state as a purely secular institution, he had already put into practice at Providence.

Disjointed and repetitious as much of it is, *The Bloudy Tenent* still followed a logical pattern because of Williams' development of the above two principles. Published anonymously, like many other similar tracts of the time, *The Bloudy Tenent* landed in the London bookstalls apparently without ever having been seen by the censor; for, had the latter merely eyed the title, he would most certainly have suppressed the edition. For the twelve statements which followed the title page would have tipped off any intelligent licenser as to the nature of the extremely inflammatory set of ideas which the work meant to consider. Of its one dozen assertions, the fifth, sixth, seventh, and eighth were typical of the contentions Williams was fervently intent upon proving:

All Civill States . . . in their respective constitutions and administration are essentially Civill, and therefore not Judges, Governours or Defendours of the Spirituall or Christian State and
Worship.

It is the will and command of God, that since the comming of
. . . the Lord Jesus a permission of the most Paganish, Jewish,
Turkish or Antichristian consciences and worships bee granted to
all men in all Nations and Countries. . . .

The state of the Land of Israel . . . is proved figurative and
ceremoniall, and no patterne or president for any Kingdom or
civill state in the world to follow.

God requireth not an uniformity of Religion to be inacted and enforced in any civill State.[25]

Here again were stated the two principles for which Williams
became famous, namely, that all men had the right to freedom of
conscience and its logical corollary that a civil government did not
have the right to impose a national church upon its citizens.

Like *Queries, The Bloudy Tenent* was dedicated to Parliament,
whose members were informed that "the greatest yoakes yet lying
upon English necks . . . are of a spirituall and soule nature," a
condition it was their duty to alleviate and not to change "the
yokes according to their consciences, Papist or Protestant . . .
which another Parliament, and the very next may turne again."
And since the parliamentarians worshipped according to their
own light, they were advised to grant the same right to others, lest
it be said at Rome and Oxford "that the Parliament of England
hath committed a greater rape, then if they had forced or ravished
the bodies of all women in the world" (9).

A note "to every Courteous Reader" indicated in the first place
that Williams thought the business of hunting down dissenters
was altogether ridiculous. In a vignette he placed Jesus and Paul
in the middle of seventeenth-century London, where both were
to denote whether it was the "Papists, Prelatists, Presbyterians
[or] Independents" they favored. Could anyone see either of these
two deeply spiritually minded men as responding "of mine, of
mine"? Furthermore, what good was it for Parliament to have

made the Bible available to Englishmen, if "against their soules perswasion from the Scriptures" they were coerced to worship "as the Church believes." In a passage vibrant with the intensity of his convictions, Williams urged his readers to regard their present religious afflictions as mere "flea-bites" and not to be deterred from their objectives, for "having bought Truth deare, we must not sell it cheap, not the least grain of it for the whole World, no not for the saving of Soules though our own most precious" (13).

The Anabaptist's letter had as its central theme "Whether Persecution for cause of Conscience be not against the Doctrine of Jesus Christ the King of Kings"; and to buttress his view, he had cited examples from the Scriptures, as well as from writers of ancient and modern history, to insist that Jesus had not come to destroy men's lives, an idea Williams also employed in his own arguments against persecution. In defense of heterodoxy, the Anabaptist had also included utterances by such contemporary rulers as James I of England and the kings of both Poland and Bohemia, all three of whom regarded their regal authority as restricted solely to their subjects' bodies.

Cotton's reply to the Anabaptist had been to the effect that no one was to be punished for his conscience, however misinformed, unless that misinformation was fundamental. In that case the misguided one had to be set straight since "in fundamental and principall points of Doctrine or Worship, the Word of God in such things is so cleare, that he cannot but bee convinced in Conscience of the dangerous Error of his way, after once or twice, Admonition wisely and faithfully dispensed" (42).

But, if anyone were not "convinced in Conscience" after these explanations, he was then ripe for punishment, and was not being "persecuted for Cause of Conscience, but for sinning against his owne Conscience." That many devout religionists were willing to suffer for their beliefs did not disturb Cotton's equanimity about the rightness of his position; these dissenters merely confirmed what the Bay understood to be true about the human condition all along; only a few were to be saved, while the great mass of mankind was doomed. Williams, agreeing with his adversary that the elect were the precious few who were to attain salvation, still took issue in his *Reply to the aforesaid Answer of Mr. Cotton in a Conference between Truth and Peace,* in which he vehemently objected to his foe's reasoning that condemned to hell-fire those who differed with him in fundamentals.

Yet so emotionally committed was Williams to his basic concept of liberty of conscience that he could not think about its defense in the form of a logical treatise. Instead, he employed the device of a dramatic colloquy between Truth and Peace, the two spokesmen who served as the favorite protagonists of the pamphleteers of the day. Unfortunately, the dialogue form gave him ample opportunity to engage in such typical excesses of style as repetition, incoherence, and his most characteristic one, "prolixitie." Despite these stylistic faults, the work reaches heights of greatness because of the intensity and force with which Williams presented his ideas.

Having presented the two views for and against persecution, Williams was quick to deny Cotton's contention that certain points of doctrine were so fundamental that "without right beliefs thereof," no one could be saved. For to agree with this premise meant to condemn to everlasting hell the many thousands of decent people who, since the death of Christ, "doe erre fundamentally concerning the true matter, constitution, gathering and governing of the Church; and yet farre be it from any pious breast to imagine that they are not saved and that their soules are not bound up in the bundle of eternal life" (64).

Himself as devout as Cotton, Williams' typological interpretation of the Bible had taught him there was not just one absolute explanation of the Scripture as the Bay would have one believe. In favoring persecution of those who "sinne against their consciences," Cotton was reminded that he was merely following in the footsteps of the Court of High Commission, and was forgetting what had been his own experience in having been expelled from England by this same court in 1633 for his dissenting views. Just as the English court needed no special reasons to defend their decision, so "Mr. Cotton measures that to others, which himselfe when he lived in such practices, would not have had measured to himself" (71).

Cotton's view of a troublesome dissenter was one who presented his beliefs in a manner that tended to disturb the civil peace; this gave Williams the opportunity to define the latter as the "pax civitatis, the peace of the Citie," which condition could be achieved in both Christian and non-Christian states alike, since it had nothing to do with religion. Also pointed out were the peaceful relations maintained in their respective areas by the colonists and the Indians "though neither in one nor the other can any man prove a true Church of God in those places, and consequently no spirituall and heavenley peace" (73, 146). This peace, moreover, was far different from the secular kind, which was "essentially civill and humane." For his differentiation between the civil and spiritual realms, Williams posited his argument on Paul's statement in 2 Corinthians 10:4 to the effect that the weapons employed in spiritual warfare were not of a material or fleshly nature.

In thus revealing the dissimilarity between the heavenly and the earthly sense of things, Williams was being the typical Puritan. But where the Bay orthodoxy thought a civil state had to be dominated by the ministry, with the magistrates serving more or less as sheriffs for the clergy, Williams was prepared to describe the essentially private role a church institution played within the organizational structure of a city:

> The Church or company of worshippers whether true or false it is like unto a Body of Colledge of Physitians in a Citie; like unto a Corporation, Society, or Company of East-Indie or Turkie-Merchants, or any other Societie or Company in London: which Companies may hold their Courts, keep their Records, hold disputations: and in matters concerning their Societie, may dissent, divide, breake into Schismes and Factions, sue and implead each other at the Law, yea wholly break up and dissolve into pieces and nothing, and yet the peace of the Citie not be in the least measure impaired or disturbed. (73)

When this concept is contrasted with the part actually played by the various Congregational Churches in the numerous settlements of the Bay where each was the dominant and unifying institution, much like the Catholic Church of Western Europe during the Middle Ages, one realizes how far apart Williams and the Bay were in their concepts of the role of the church in the community. In Massachusetts, there were only Congregational Churches, whose supremacy the civil magistrates were pledged to defend; but, in Rhode Island, Anglicans, Baptists, Antinomians, Seekers, and later Quakers and Jews were free to worship their respective faiths with no interference from the authorities. As for Cotton's

thesis for persecution, not "one tittle" did Williams find in the
Bible to support it; and he consequently implored the Boston minister to be gentle to all persons, Christians and non-Christians
alike; especially to Jews and Turks and pagans was Cotton to be
compassionate, since "out of them Gods elect may be called to the
fellowship of Christ Jesus" (92–3). This idea of an open-door policy to win over converts to Christianity was altogether at variance
with that of the Bay, where only Puritan Congregationalists were
regarded as true Christians.

Because of their different concepts on what constituted a true
church and a godly membership, an understanding of Cotton's
and Williams' interpretations of the parable of the tares as nar-
rated in Matthew 13 is necessary. In this apologue, one may re-
call, once the good seed was sown both wheat and tares sprang
up, with the latter burned at harvest time, which period symbolized the end of the world. For Cotton and the other Bay ministers,
the tares signified either the hypocrites who managed to become
members of the churches and were "like unto the godly," or corrupt doctrines and practices, "yet such as come very near the
Truth as Tares do to the Wheat" (97). To Williams, on the other
hand, these same tares represented outright "Antichrist idolaters,"
while for both ministers the wheat symbolized truly devout Christians.

For his disagreement with the Bay concept, Williams drew on
his knowledge of Greek to show that tares meant nothing more
than weeds, cockle, darnell—in short, a kind of chaff as far removed from wheat as one could imagine. Thus hypocrites, unlike
the truly godlike, he contended, could by their very nature be
detected and ousted from their places in church. But, in accord
with his distinction between the spiritual and civil realms, the
hypocrites, "who labour spiritually to devoure the flock and to
draw away Disciples after them," were to be allowed to live in the
world and "no carnall force . . . to be used against them." When
the harvest time came, they would obtain their just deserts (99–
100).

Cotton's position on the difficulty of detecting hypocrites, however, was not without good reason for Bay purposes. For, if religious deceivers managed to fool the very elect in Massachusetts,
how very right, then, it was for the saints to punish actual dissenters and nonconformists like Williams whose openly plied

views on Separatism were regarded as heretical. Could anyone then point a finger at the oligarchy as persecutors if the brethren were concerned solely with punishing openly declared trouble-makers? But to Williams, the Bay elect, in uprooting those whom they regarded as idolatrous, were acting contrary to the commands of Jesus. For in the process of persecution, "Gods people the good wheat hath also been pluckt up, as all Ages and Histories testifie, and too too oft the World laid upon bloody heapes in civill and intestine desolations . . . (17). This desolation could have been avoided had Jesus' command been obeyed, "to wit, to let them alone untill the Harvest."

For Williams there was yet another reason why religious hypo-crites were not to be punished by the civil authorities. By virtue of their hopelessly benighted state, they were already "stark blinde" and deprived of spiritual understanding. For these forsaken ones, a sense of compassion was certainly necessary, since their fate was "ever-lasting burnings" in the bottomless pit which separated evil-doers from God. Again, one did not have to fear that these sinners could injure the civil state, since this institution, "being in a natu-rall state dead in sin," was incapable of additional infection (125–126). In holding this concept, Williams of course differed from the Bay elect who felt it their duty to guide, via their magistrates, those already damned. Again, as far as he was concerned, there was no need to punish anyone for spiritual offenses, for fear that there was no other way of handling these transgressions. As head of the church, Jesus had not at all been "unfaithfull in providing antitodes and preservatives against the spirituall sicknesses . . . of his Church and people."

For Williams, too, the chief reason England had undergone so many switches from Catholicism to Protestantism was that each time a new monarch came to the throne, he could buttress his faith by the "stronger Sword" he had operating in his behalf against his opponents. The end result, however, of enforcing con-formity to the state religion was to inculcate a sense of hypocrisy, for those so coerced soon realized that "that Religion cannot be true which needs such instruments to uphold it." Moreover, to appreciate how atypical the Bay situation was with its close spirit-ual and civil ties, Williams maintained that during the seven-teenth century many countries throughout the world practiced separation of church and state. In such lands non-Christians were allowed to worship their respective faiths; and as long as they obeyed the civil laws they were not molested, although by ordinary Christian standards their spiritual practices might have been considered wolfish. By the same token, hypocrites who were intent upon subverting the teachings of true religion in either Christian or non-Christian countries were also not to be punished as long as they were obedient to civil rulers. They were not to be molested because Christ never gave civil magistrates orders to interfere in spiritual matters, and nowhere in the New Testament did Jesus ever "joyne to His Breastplate of Righteousnesse, the breastplate of iron and steel" (149).

Another example of the disparate manner in which both Cotton and Williams regarded the office of the civil magistrate was seen in their respective interpretations of Romans 13. Cotton, who had used the text dealing with the subjection of citizens to their magistrates as one of his bases for persecution, claimed that civil officers were responsible for the enforcement of both Tables: the first four commandments, which pertained to one's duties to God as well as with the last six, which were concerned with man's responsibilities toward his fellow men. Williams, on the other hand, interpreted the chapter to mean obedience to the authorities in civil matters alone, and to reinforce his contention employed statements by Calvin and Beza, Calvin's illustrious follower in Geneva, in which the jurisdiction of the magistrate was seen as "essentially civill."

The harrassment of the minds and bodies of dissenters was but one great injustice in a close church-state relationship. A second wrong, Williams believed, was the taxing of these same nonconformists for the support of this church: "Who knowes not what constraint lies upon all consciences in Old and New England, to come to Church, and pay Church duties . . ." (194). And despite denials by Cotton on this score, testimony by Winthrop and Lechford afford evidence that, except for Boston, all Bay residents, whether churchgoers or not, were taxed for the ministers' maintenance—hence the opportunity for civil interference in church affairs. Together with this need to tax nearly everyone, Williams also saw the reason why other denominations were excluded from the Bay: the loss of revenue that would take place as such denominations used their church collections for their own purposes. To Williams it was manifestly clear that the Bay ministers would never have called upon the magistrates if they were certain of having "the same supply of maintainance without the helpe of the Civil Sword, or were persuaded to live upon the voluntary contribution of poore Saints, or their own labour . . ." (194, 283, 395–96).

Still, forcing people to pay for the upkeep of the ministry was one thing; compelling them to worship at the state church was another, one which indicated a complete inability to realize that a national church was "not the Institution of the Lord Jesus Christ." For the Hebrews a state church had been mandated by God, and this form of government had served them admirably; but to Williams with his typological reasoning, this type of church had been abolished at the coming of Christ. Moreover "the particular Churches of Christ in all part of the world" under the Congregational form of discipline needed no help at present from a material sword but were able instead to defend themselves by the sword of spirit. Therefore, magistrates who intervened in matters of conscience had to possess authorization from Christ Jesus "to determine in all the great controversies concerning doctrine, discipline, government"—an office Christ had definitely not given them (201).

Once more freedom of conscience was urged in behalf of Catholics, and in so doing, Williams indicated that persecution for conscience' sake could cease—were the persecutor himself aware of man's erring tendencies and limitations. Perhaps "our owne mistakes and ignorance, the sense of our own weaknesses and blindnesse . . . and the great professed expectation of light to come which we are not now able to comprehend, may abate the edge, yea sheath up the sword of persecution toward any . . ." (206).

Profoundly certain of the need for more light in working out his own salvation but also assured that his Calvinistic theology suited his spiritual needs, Williams was never authoritarian in the sense that Cotton was who thought that his way was the only one of attaining salvation. And, from the vantage point of his deep spiritual cast of thought, Williams' insight into the human condition was simple and clear-cut: the inhabitants of this world were either spiritually dead or alive. If dead in sin, then no one could kill them, no more than a dead man could be killed. If spiritually alive, however, it was neither false religions nor false teachers, whom Cotton was so intent upon persecuting, which prevented the attainment of true salvation; it was two other matters: the forcing of consciences to worship a state or national religion, and the engaging in civil strife to defend one's religion and perhaps dying before one could gain repentance (208).

Williams agreed with Cotton that only those who truly feared God should enjoy liberty of conscience. But in light of the many controversies relating to the true church, his query was—who was to be judge in this matter? Over this issue of judging godliness of character, Williams related a telling example of Bay intolerance. Some English Presbyterians, contemplating migration to New England, had written to the Bay ministers for answers to thirty-two questions relating to church doctrine. Their thirty-first query —could they enjoy religious liberty in New England while practicing their own church discipline—was answered with an un-equivocal *No!* Because the Presbyterians practiced a different form of church constitution, the Bay "could not approve their Civill cohabitation with them, and consequently could not advise the Magistrates to suffer them to enjoy a Civill being within this Jurisdicton" (215–16).

This despite the fact that the Bay ministers readily acknowl-edged their questioners to be a godly people and suggested, that once arrived in New England, a rapprochement would probably take place with the Congregationalists either winning the new set-tlers over to their church doctrine or vice versa. And ostensibly to show how truly humble and humane they really were, the Bay ministers, with Cotton as their spokesman, insisted that they had never set themselves up as paragons of perfection, since men were by nature weak and could not dream of perfection in this life.

This last admission, seemingly modest and meek, Williams flung back into Cotton's teeth; how could this be an honest state-ment of Bay weakness "when they preach, print and practice such violence to the soules and bodies of others, and by their Rules and Grounds ought to proceed even to the killing of those whom they judge so deare unto them, and in respect of godlinesse far above themselves" (217)?

With this outburst of the difference between the Bay's apparent position of humility and its actual performance, the colloquy be-tween Truth and Peace ended. Once more Williams' hammer blows had pounded home the fact that, as long as people within a state did not disturb the civil peace, their religious beliefs were their own business, an idea which has worked successfully in all Western countries where people have had a voice in their own governments.

Still left for Truth and Peace to discuss was *A Model of Church and Civil Power*, which Williams thought Cotton had written since this treatise so clearly reflected the Bostonian's views on the intervention of the civil magistrate to stamp out incipient schisms and heresies; in point of fact, the *Model* had been written by the associated ministers of the Bay. Concerned with the furor caused by Williams' sentence of expulsion and the acceptance of his unorthodox ideas by many members of the Salem congregation, these ministers sought to consolidate their forces against any further outbreaks of heresy. That there was nothing in the tenets of Congregationalism that allowed one church to interfere in the internal affairs of another did not deter the oligarchy; these men were as certain of their stand for Nonseparation as Williams was for his of Separatism; consequently, they felt justified in intervening whenever heresy or schism, as they understood these terms, cropped up.

Oddly enough, it was not the ministers who initiated the idea for the *Model* but the magistrates, who, in order to proceed against Williams in 1635, suggested that the clergy draw "one uniforme order of dissipline in the churches" so that the magistrates would know how far they were "bound to interpose for the preservation of that uniformity." [26] That the magistrates should have sought help from the elders in running their affairs was not extraordinary. Fashioned on the Mosaic commonwealth of the Hebrews, the Bay government rested on the laws of the Bible as much as it did on the charter granted them by Charles I. Hence it was natural that in troublesome matters of state, the magistrates would look to the elders for an elucidation of the Scriptures. In return for this help, the magistrates expressed their gratitude by serving as the guardians of the orthodoxy that the oligarchy wished to keep intact.

Thus came about the *Model*, or the ministerial review of the respective roles the churches and civil officers played in the affairs of the colony, and of those areas where the civil arm could be expected to intervene in church matters. Evolving as sixteen "heads" or questions, the first few centered on such matters as the

manner in which church and state might stand together; the supe-
riority of one sphere over the other; the objectives of each sphere
and the proper means whereby each could attain its respective
ends. Four other "heads" related to the power the magistrates possessed in the making of laws; the subjection of the churches to
these legislative enactments; the punishment to be accorded
churches breaking these laws; and the power the magistrate had
in the gathering or forming of churches. Four of the remaining
questions were concerned with the magistrate's powers in church
matters: in providing the churches with their officers; in matters
of doctrine and of worship; in censure of the churches, and in
keeping the churches from assembling publicly. The authority the
particular churches had over the magistrates; the various reasons
whereby churches could proceed against magistrates in matters of
offense; and the magistrates' power "in the Liberties and Privi-
ledges of these Churches" constituted the final three "heads."

In Williams' denunciation of magisterial intervention in purely
religious affairs, he again drew abundant examples from the
Scriptures and English history to expose the falsity of the *Model*'s
reasoning. And where the strength of his earlier attack against
Cotton's policy of persecution had been in his understanding that
Jesus had never used force to convert people to Christianity, in his
assault on the *Model*, he based his argument on the fact that Jesus
never called upon the civil authorities to help him run his church.

Once again Williams reiterated his position that the civil government, while "an Ordinance of God," had only the power given
it by the people; therefore, the magistrate's authority was only a
delegated one. Again, the election of magistrates by the people
also made it incongruous for these officials to interfere in church
affairs. For, in so doing, they assumed that the people fundamentally and originally had the power, among other things, to govern
the church—an absurdity Williams thought so grotesque as to pull
Christ and God out of heaven and "subject them unto naturall,
sinful, inconstant man, and so consequently to Sathan Himselfe."
Under such an administration there would be no God worshipped
"according to the institutions of Christ Jesus except the severall
peoples of the Nations of the World shall give allowance." 27

Disorganized and rambling as Williams was in *The Bloudy
Tenent*, there was no mistaking the basic intent of the work. To
the Presbyterians in the Assembly, for whom a stable national

order was largely dependent on instituting a united comprehensive church, the tract was anathema chiefly for the many reasons Williams set forth against such an establishment. Consequently, it was no surprise that Parliament had the essay burned, finding its chief fault to be "the tolerating of all Sorts of Religion." [28] Typical of the attack made by those who found the tract utterly abhorrent was that of William Prynne, one of the most bigoted and fanatical of the Presbyterians, who called the work a "dangerous Licentious Booke." In his *Twelve Considerable Serious Questions touching Church Government,* Prynne had joined in the attack against the Independent ministers for their *Apologeticall Narration,* and had stated that the kind of toleration desired by the five dissenting brethren would result in all types of error and lawlessness. His eleventh question inquired whether Williams was not in effect requesting that everyone of whatever sect or creed "be left free to his owne free liberty of conscience" and thus be permitted to take in any "false, seditious, detestable" belief he might embrace. After alluding to Richard Overton's pamphlet on *Mans Mortallitie* and to Milton's tract on the *Doctrine and Discipline of Divorce*—subjects deemed reprehensible at the time by the Presbyterians who characterized them as typical of the corruption which came with the failure to reform the church on Presbyterian lines—Prynne added *The Bloudy Tenent* to his list of works which tended to "the late dangerous increase of many Anabaptisticall, Antinomian, Hereticall, Atheisticall opinions. . . ." [29]

Williams' own reasoning can be used to contain or greatly minimize Prynne's onslaught. Certain as Williams was that no true church had existed since the Apostasy, he could not see people being coerced into worshipping in a national church, which to him was the embodiment of the Antichrist. Better by far, if men were left free to seek truth by the best light they had, just as they were doing in Rhode Island, with no coercion on the part of the civil magistrate. Furthermore, it was his ardent belief that what might appear to be atheistical or heretical opinions to the orthodoxy, might very well appear to be bona fide truth to the so-called heretics entertaining them; for even in religious fundamentals people could be wrong. Furthermore, what might be deemed right religious practice for one age might be termed false in the next; but, so long as they obeyed the civil laws, earnest religionists were to be allowed to worship according to their light.

Influential as *The Bloudy Tenent* has been from the time it was written in determining the views of many on religious liberty and the dissociation of church and state, these ideas were not new for their day. Many of the sects, especially the Anabaptists, had entertained these same concepts earlier than Williams, who in fact was greatly indebted to their tracts for some of his thoughts. In its own day, however, only four years after it was written, there is ample testimony available of the influence of Williams' tract on the English Revolution of 1648, when the Levellers, aided by their leaders John Lilburne and William Walwynn, actually plumped for a democratic government in which the common people of England could participate.[30] In fact, from 1643 to 1649, more than one hundred and twenty pamphlets appeared, which either attacked or defended Williams; and, besides Prynne, among his more important detractors were David Stewart, Hugh Peters, Robert Baillie, and Thomas Edwards—all of whom wrote scathingly of the Rhode Islander's insistence that liberty of conscience was an absolute right and that the source of all government lay in the hands of the people. On the other hand, among the more popular defenses of *The Bloudy Tenent* and from which the author quoted extensively was Richard Overton's *The Araignment of Mr. Persecution,* printed in April, 1645, which satirized the Presbyterians and their goal of an established church.[31]

In time the idea that all political power lay with the people did catch on, as did the idea of religious liberty. The Constitution of the United States solemnly asserts the first fact in its preamble; the right to worship according to one's own light is guaranteed in the First Amendment.

## V  Christenings Make Not Christians

*The Bloudy Tenent* concluded Williams' major blast against religious intolerance. Making for a change of theme was the last tract he published entitled *Christenings Make Not Christians.*[32] Appearing on the London bookstalls in January, 1645, long after he had returned to Providence, the slender twenty-one-page pamphlet reverted to the subject of conversion which Williams had initially discussed in the *Key.* In that work, he had promised "a briefe Additional discourse" on the subject; and this promise *Christenings Make Not Christians* attempted to fulfill.

One reason Williams had given in the *Key* for not having worked more earnestly at Christianizing the natives was that no true conversions could be effected where there was no genuine penitence on the part of the would-be converts. It remained for this last work, however, to furnish still other reasons for his Laodicean attitude, but not before he had expressed some sharp truths relevant to a true sense of Christianity, which would tend only to exacerbate his fellow Puritans in Massachusetts whom he found wanting in this respect.

The full title of the work—*Christenings Make Not Christians or a Briefe Discourse concerning that name Heathen, commonly given to the Indians, also concerning that great point of their Conversion*—made clear the material he meant to consider. He had employed the term *heathen* in *The Bloudy Tenent* and had also shown that the Bay theocrats used the word to include not only the naked savages of North America, but also those peoples, both ancient and modern, who were "not the Church and people of God in Christ." [33] This designation of the unclad Indians as heathens seemed improper and unchristian to Williams, whose knowledge of Hebrew and Greek supplied the information that the word merely refered to those gentiles and nations who were outside the national church of the Jews, who of all nations in their day were alone God's people.[34]

But, true to his sense of typology that God had repudiated the Jews with the advent of Jesus, Williams believed that for his day the only people of God, in the sense that they were a chosen generation as set forth in 1 Peter 2:9, were the Christians (32). This conclusion had been reached in accord with the stipulation in the text of 1 Corinthians 5 that all peoples had to be classified as dwelling either within or without the church of God. But because of a map of one Herdious, who had labeled as Christian the continents of Asia and Europe, as well as large parts of Africa and America, Williams found that "Without is turned to be Within, [and all] the World turned Christian."

And because this geographical assessment automatically converted everyone in the then known world to Christianity, he felt impelled to define anew what the two terms Christ and Christians meant to him. The former he defined as the anointed one of God, whom the kings, prophets, and priests of Israel "did prefigure and type out," whereas Christians were those who followed "the

anointed one in all his Offices." But since the Scriptures had nothing to say about the world become "christian, holy, anointed,
Gods People," Williams declared Herdious' concept false (33).
He was also certain it was not the entire world the mapmaker
meant to designate as Christian, but only those lands and countries over which the Roman church ruled, the same Papacy referred to in the thirteenth chapter of Revelation as the beast and
later as the Antichrist; for these followers of the Papacy, William
felt Christ had prepared a drink from "the dreadfullest cup that
the whole Booke of God ever held forth to sinners."

Further discussion of the term *heathen* on Williams' part revealed that the word did not apply solely to gentiles and nations
outside the true church; it also referred to those nations who had
broken away from the Catholic yoke and had become Protestant,
but who were still in opposition to what really constituted God's
people in that they had not come out "from ANTICHRISTIAN abominations, from his markes in a false conversion, and a false constitution, or framing of NATIONAL CHURCHES in false MINISTERIES and
ministrations of BAPTISME . . ." (34).

Here of course was a direct hit at the Bay and its Nonseparatist
policy in regard to the Anglican Church. And, since they tolerated
these heathenish conditions, Protestants were urged to consider
how deeply they had emerged from "that Beast and his Pisture," a
matter that concerned "each soule to search into." Furthermore, in
calling themselves *Christians,* while simultaneously pursuing
church forms "drawn after Romes pattern," the Bay Puritans were
seen as "no more Christian [than] the name"; they were not better in fact than the Indians whose sins fell "far short of European
sinners." In equating the Bay settlers with the natives, Williams
was merely acting in accord with his conviction that, since Christ's
coming, all mankind was the handiwork of God, who was no re-
specter of persons (35).

On the subject of conversions, Williams discounted Catholic
claims to great success in these endeavors in Canada, Maryland,
and the West Indies. The Antichrist being their "false head,"
Catholic teachings, preachings, and conversions were for him, of
necessity, false. And while he could easily "have brought the whole
[Narragansett] country to have observed one day in seven" and
have them undergo baptism and attend church, so much did they
respect and admire him, to have done so, however, would have

been against his principles. For it would have called "that conversion unto God, which is indeed subversion of the soules of Millions in Christendome, from one false worship to another, and the prophanation of the holy name of God, his holy Son and blessed Ordinance" (37). The claims of the Bay to great numbers of conversions, Williams also discounted on the basis that, once having made the natives conform to Christian teachings and think of themselves as a transformed people, the Bay ministers still went about catching them "by an after conversion." It was this twofold method of Christianization that troubled him (37).

In summing up his feelings about false conversions, Williams listed five examples whereby this type could be recognized, the first four of which expressed actions which revealed their practitioners to be far from the true God. The fifth illustration, wherein people were forced to worship as the civil sword dictated, was deemed the most heinous of all and one Jesus never ordered, his compelling coming about solely "by the mighty perswasions of his Messengers."

True conversions, on the other hand, were to be distinguished by the following criteria: they had to be similar to those performed in Jesus' day; and they had to be effected by messengers, who, while preaching repentance and proclaiming forgiveness, had to also prove they were sent by the Master Christian to do this work. Again, truly spiritual reformation succeeded in turning the whole man from Satan to God and in replacing idol worship with holy worship.

As has already been noted, in his inability to "pretend a false conversion, and false sense of worship, to the true Jesus," lay one cause for Williams' lukewarm attitude to this aspect of the ministry. There were also other reasons; one was the language barrier, a problem which made "propriety of speech to open matters of salvation" to the natives difficult for him. But for one who had spent a good many years studying the various Indian dialects in order to compile the words and phrases for the *Key*, the linguistic obstacle was not an insuperable one. His failure to work more earnestly at conversion lay in his doubt that he had ever been commissioned or authorized by God to perform this work. For him there could be no true preaching without a true sending, as outlined in Matthew 28; and in this regard he was deeply concerned where "that power now lyes" (41). Another assailing doubt was whether the battle between Christ and the Antichrist did not first have to be fought and won before "the law and word of life" could be sent to those parts of the earth where the name of Christ had not yet been heard.

As for the many Catholics and Protestants who claimed to have been truly sent to engage in the work of conversion, Williams was not presently concerned with them. At some future time he would address some queries to them which would fill them with shame and make them realize that, in having preached without a commission from the Lord, they had engaged "in whorish worships." Some seven years later, in 1652 to be exact, in *The Hireling Ministry None of Christs* he was to give a fuller account of his position on conversion and the basis for "a true Commission for such an Embassie and Ministry."

CHAPTER *4*

# Works Published in England, 1652

WILLIAMS' second voyage to England in 1651 was occasioned by the failure of the 1644 charter to effect the desired unity of Rhode Island, where disaffection continued to plague the colony even though a central government had been instituted in 1647. Among those who stood to gain most by keeping Rhode Island disunited was Massachusetts who, through her hegemony in the United Colonies, pursued policies intended to humble Williams' long-time friends and allies, the Narragansetts.[1] In the efforts of the Narragansetts to assert leadership over the Mohegans, one of their tributary tribes, they were constantly harassed by Bay practices which enabled the Mohegans to murder Miantonomu, the leader of the Narragansetts, and yet remain free from their Indian overlords. Williams' intervention several times from 1644 to 1650 as mediator and negotiator between the Bay and the Narragansetts, who were intent upon obtaining revenge for the murder of their sachem, more than once prevented outright war and its consequent havoc in the Narragansett Bay area.

Humiliating the Narragansetts, however, was but one aspect of the Bay design to keep the heretical colony weak. Intent upon wiping out what could be termed "the Rhode Island way of life," the Bay saints had never honored Williams' patent and had insisted that the spurious charter their agent Thomas Weld managed to obtain in 1645 gave them suzerainty over Providence and Aquidneck.[2] Nor did Massachusetts lack for confederates from within Williams' colony who were intent upon keeping him from effectively consolidating its various settlements. One such was William Arnold whose greed for ever greater tracts of land had caused him to leave Providence for Pawtuxet in 1638. He was soon instrumental in bringing this new area under Bay jurisdiction, whose magistrates allowed him to run it unmolested by Rhode Island authority. In the meantime, Arnold constantly advised the saints to absorb additional areas; finally in May, 1650, Massachusetts incorporated Pawtuxet and Warwick into its own Suffolk county.[3]

This action was taken despite the fact that Warwick, where the followers of Samuel Gorton had finally settled after they had been forced to leave Pawtuxet because of Arnold's designs on their land, had apparently won their battle to live undisturbed as a result of Gorton's successful trip to England in 1645. There the fiery champion of English civil law in his pamphlet, *Simplicities Defence*, exposed the persecution and land-grabbing policies of the saints, as a result of which the Council of State ordered the Bay to allow the Gortonists "freely and quietly to live and plant upon Shawomett," [4] whose name was soon changed to Warwick in gratitude for the new charter.

In April, 1651, came word that Coddington had obtained a commission in England which made him governor for life of Aquidneck, a decision which in effect totally nullified Williams' charter. A separate settlement over which Coddington alone could govern had been his desire for years, his aristocratic leanings from the start having made him contemptuous of the political democracy Williams had sought to build. To revoke this newly granted commission, the dissatisfied freemen of Aquidneck, who wanted no part of Coddington's feudal order, authorized John Clarke, a Baptist minister and physician from Newport, to leave for England and to present their case before the Council of State. The summer prior to his departure, Clarke had figured in a case of persecution in which Endecott, Williams' warm friend during his Salem days, acted the persecutor. As a consequence, Williams sent his old friend a blistering letter in which he reminded Endecott of their former relationship, and also inquired whether "no Consciences [were] to breathe the Aire, but such as suit and sample his?" [5]

Clarke's role in the above episode had come about as a result of his having gone off with two fellow Baptists from Rhode Island, Obadiah Holmes and John Crandall, to visit Lynn, Massachusetts, where a member of their sect was ill. There, because of a sermon Clarke preached denying infant baptism—then the most controversial issue in the Bay churches—the three were apprehended and sentenced to be whipped unless they paid heavy fines. Because friends paid the sum assessed against him, Clarke escaped the lash; not so lucky was Holmes, who was cruelly scourged.

Clarke later wrote of the incident in his *Ill Newes from New England*, which appeared in London in May, 1652, and which won to his side many in the mother country who had become increasingly disenchanted with the persecution tactics of the Massachusetts saints. Clarke had left for England in November, 1651, with Williams, who had been pressured by the freemen of Warwick and Providence into accompanying the Baptist minister (whose mission he was to aid), but who had also recognized his opportunity in this second trip abroad to have the 1644 charter confirmed. And, despite a growing family to care for, he again put the welfare of the colony first. Selling his trading post at Cocumcussot, a few miles from Providence, in order to obtain money for his passage, he and Clarke arrived in London early in 1652.

A letter William Arnold wrote the Bay governor upon learning that Williams was considering accompanying Clarke is indicative of the deep hatred and animosity borne by those who wished to see the Rhode Island experiment destroyed. Urging the oligarchs to seize Providence immediately, this ancestor of traitor Benedict Arnold also warned them that, were Clarke and Williams successful in obtaining a new charter, Rhode Island would continue to remain a sanctuary where "under the pretence of liberty of conscience about these partes there comes to live all the scume . . . of the country." [6] There was of course some truth in Arnold's assertion, for many who came to Rhode Island in the name of religion mistook liberty of conscience for license.

In the meantime, across the Atlantic, Williams saw in 1652 an England far different from the one he had visited in 1643. The Civil War had ended in a complete victory for the Independents, with Cromwell having emerged as their leader. However, the beheading of Charles by the Puritans in 1649 had caused a revulsion among many of his previous subjects; hitherto favorably disposed to the victors, many Englishmen now felt that a sacrilegious act had been perpetrated. To further complicate matters, as a result of the liberty they had enjoyed after the war, the many and various sectaries grew increasingly clamorous for greater toleration— a situation that caused Cromwell to tread gingerly among them, divided as they were by the two major disparate political and social ideals which the revolution had brought in its wake. The first, a purely democratic concept, emphasized the equality of all believers. As preached by John Lilburne and William Walwynn, the leaders of the Levellers, who were newly arrived on the political scene, this idea had its genesis among the common soldiers who had fought under Cromwell. And it was for these average Englishmen that Lilburne and Walwynn sought more political rights than they had previously enjoyed.

In direct contrast to this leveling tendency was the concept of the elect—the spiritual elite upon whom devolved the responsibility of governing the mass of mankind—which was unavoidably in conflict with the reasoning behind the equality of all believers. While Cromwell was a religious liberal and wholeheartedly for the toleration of all sects, including the newly emerged and raucous Quakers, he, by virtue of his early background as a country squire, sided politically with the many conservative Puritans who favored a social hierarchy in which the chosen few governed the multitudes. Not until the nineteenth century, when the demands of the Chartists were gradually made part of their political life, did Englishmen begin to enjoy the kind of democracy envisioned by Lilburne and Walwynn.

Once arrived in the mother country and intent upon completing his mission as rapidly as possible, Williams early sought out his old friend, Henry Vane, a member of the Council of State, the group that served as the executive branch of the Commonwealth which Cromwell had helped to establish following the execution of Charles. Composed of a rump Parliament whose approval of measures was virtually guaranteed once the Council of State, who were also members of Parliament, gave its imprimatur, the Commonwealth served as England's government from 1649 to April, 1653. Then, tired of the restraints parliamentary government imposed upon him, Cromwell dissolved the rump and instituted the Protectorate.[7] But in early 1652 the Council of State was to stand Williams in good stead. For besides Vane, other important members of this body included Sir William Masham, Cornelius Holland, and Cromwell himself, all of them tried and true friends who could be counted upon to help him to have the 1644 charter confirmed. Cromwell, for example, though busy with affairs of state and of religion, still managed to hold "many discourses" with Williams on the re-entry of the Jewish people into England and on the complaint made by the Narragansetts against the Bay because of the latter's promise to war against them unless they embraced Christianity.[8]

Early in April, with the aid of Vane whom he termed "the sheet-anchor of our ship," Williams placed his case before the Council; but his objective was temporarily stymied by the outbreak of war between Holland and England. Hence not until October 2 was Coddington's commission revoked and the 1644 charter confirmed. As Coddington's warrant had been based on the fraudulent claim that he had discovered and bought Aquidneck for his own use, Williams had no trouble disproving it since he had written the Aquidneck deed himself and had been one of the two English witnesses to sign it.[9] A new charter was what Williams really wanted, since it would have given Rhode Island the backing of the Commonwealth, but this was not to be so easily obtained. For, besides the Bay, Plymouth and Connecticut had also laid claims to Rhode Island territory; and their agents in London were just as astute and influential with the various Council members as Williams was. Sir Arthur Haselrig, for example, who had previously helped Williams to obtain the 1644 patent, as a member of the Council in 1652 backed the claims of his son-in-law Colonel George Fenwick, who happened to be one of Connecticut's two agents.

On September 8, 1652, Williams had written home that it would be some time before the controversy over the charter would end.[10] He had further indicated that he meant to institute a lawsuit against his brother Robert over the nonpayment of funds as commanded in their mother's will; as a consequence, he could not see himself leaving England until the spring of 1654. When he did in fact return to Providence in February of that year, Clarke was left to carry on negotiations for a new charter. What with various changes in government, begun first by Cromwell and then later by the English in restoring Charles II to the throne, eleven long years were to elapse before Rhode Island obtained its second patent in 1663 from the restored Stuart ruler.

When not concerned with charters and lawsuits, Williams made judicious use of his time, renewing acquaintanceships and making new friends among the brilliant members of the group in which Vane traveled and to which he introduced him. Two new friends he made at this time were Sir Henry Lawrence, president of the State Council, and Major-General Harrison, the leader of the Fifth Monarchy men, the most radical sect produced by the revolution. Believing as they did that the four temporal monarchies of the world had passed away and that the fifth, that of God's saints, was about to begin as the immediate preliminary to the Second Coming of Christ or the millennium, Harrison's followers were ready to initiate their reign with direct military action. While acknowledging the worthiness of Harrison himself, Williams, with his hatred of compulsion in spirituals, felt the man to be altogether too "high flown for the kingdome of the saints." [11]

Charles Vane, Colonel Danvers, and Major Butler were some others he met, and he immediately cooperated with them by editing a small pamphlet on the subject of toleration. Williams' connection with Milton also dates from this period, though it is difficult to believe that the two men had not met through Vane, whom both knew, during the Rhode Islander's first trip abroad. In any event, with the Dutch war going on, Milton, now Secretary of Foreign Tongues under the Commonwealth and already partially blind, made practical use of his new friend's ability as a linguist; for, as Williams later wrote, for the "Dutch I read him, [Milton] read me many more languages." [12] These two great protagonists for freedom of thought must surely have engaged in some stimulating conversations when they got to know each other better, yet one would venture to say that Milton, Renaissance humanist that he was, would have been less concerned with church matters than his friend, and more concerned with the need to free men's minds from error and superstition.

The letter mentioning the friendship between the two Puritans also shed light on the manner Williams made ends meet, since his townsmen sent him only eighteen pounds for maintenance while he was abroad.[13] In instructing the two sons of a parliamentarian at a time when grammar rules were "esteemed a tyranny" because of Comenius' contemporaneous educational theories, Williams quickly revealed that his too was a practical approach, teaching his charges "as we teach our children English, by words, phrases and constant talk." [14]

In his efforts to renew friendships, the spring of 1652 found Williams corresponding with Mrs. Anne Sadleir, the daughter of his old patron, Sir Edward Coke. The three letters each wrote the other are important for highlighting the religious differences between the orthodox view represented by Coke's daughter and the open-ended approach taken by Williams. Wishing to pay his respects to Mrs. Sadleir and "to that blessed root" from which she sprang, he sent with his first letter a copy of *Experiments of Spiritual Life and Health,* a small devotional work he had just published; and he notified her that his present intentions were similar to those he entertained in 1644: to contend for "the true ministry of Christ and the soul freedoms of the people." [15] For his pains, Mrs. Sadleir, like her father a staunch defender of the Anglican Church, advised him that at present she was not reading as much as she used to; she did mention, however, a few works written by Anglican ministers whom she thought he might profit by. These included Bishop Andrewes' sermons, Jeremy Taylor's works, and Hooker's *Ecclesiastical Polity.* Also mentioned was the *Eikon Basilike,* a tract supposedly written by Charles I, and which concerned itself with his last days. These texts constituted her spiritual guides; and, as for her correspondent's "new lights" which he was so busy turning on, she would not be surprised if they turned out to be "but dark lanterns." [16]

Exacerbated by the last remark and at his controversial best when confronted by a viewpoint differing from his own, Williams responded by promising to read the works recommended by her. She was to do likewise with a copy of *The Bloody Tenent Yet More Bloody,* which he had just published, in which his aim was to prove "that in soul matters no weapons but soul weapons are reaching and effectual." In answering him, Mrs. Sadleir voiced her utter repugnance to the idea that men should be free to embrace whatever faith appealed to them and simultaneously acknowledged her gratitude to her parents for having reared her in the Anglican faith, "the old and best religion." [17]

In his final letter Williams asserted that until he had been enlightened otherwise by God, he too had been reared in the Anglican faith. He also took the opportunity to denounce hireling ministers of whatever faith as false prophets and teachers, for true ministers of Christ were volunteers "born of his Spirit." He had read the books she recommended, and in turn he advised her to run through Taylor's *Liberty of Prophesying,* where she would find the great Anglican preacher taking his stand for toleration, including the right of Catholics to worship freely.

Nothing he had written up to this point would have infuriated Mrs. Sadleir as much as his reaction to *Eikon Basilike.* Stigmatizing Charles as "vicious, a swearer from his youth, and an oppressor and persecutor of good men," he bade her obtain a copy of

Milton's *Eikonoklastes* for a true portrait of the late Stuart ruler. In a bitterly stinging reply which was to end the correspondence once and for all, she accused Williams of having a "face of brass"; furthermore his denunciation of Charles had not surprised her because history revealed that good kings were always subject to calumination. As for Milton, Charles's denigrator, God had certainly punished him by making him blind. As far as she was concerned, Taylor's *Liberty of Prophesying*, together with Williams, "would make a good fire." [18]

As in his first trip abroad, Williams again published five works. *The Bloody Tenent Yet More Bloody* and *Experiments of Spiritual Life and Health*, both came off the press the same April he started negotiations for the confirmation of his charter; three other tracts he wrote this same busy spring which concerned themselves with urgent contemporary issues were *The Examiner Defended*, *A Hireling Ministry None of Christs*, and *The Fourth Paper Presented by Major Butler*.

## I  The Fourth Paper Presented by Major Butler

Two major problems which the Commonwealth soon faced came ironically enough as a result of the victory over Charles. The first, in the religious sphere, was concerned with the increasing clamor of the sects for greater toleration. The second, in the political realm, was the concern felt by most orthodox Puritans at the efforts of the Levellers to assume a greater role in running the government. In this situation Cromwell's contradictory personality was exposed to full view. Ever the champion of religious reform, yet because of his desire for a stratified society where the economically and socially privileged elect were to rule the many, it was simply a matter of time before he would find the equalitarian views of the Levellers politically repugnant; and in July, 1653, he in fact imprisoned Lilburne for advocating free government. This action, coupled with his dissolution of the rump the same year and the establishment of the Protectorate, served to bring full circle his hatred of the Leveller kind of democracy and temporarily halted further political reforms.

On the religious front, the publication in February, 1652, of John Biddle's edition of *The Racovian Catechism*, with its Socinian leanings toward the innate goodness of man, brought the whole matter of toleration to a head. Angry at the attack on Calvin's doctrine of natural depravity, some twenty-six Independent ministers led by John Owen, who once had been Cromwell's chaplain, and whose ear he still commanded, were successful in having Biddle's edition burned in April by order of Parliament.[19]

An even more significant result of the Socinian heresy, however, was the establishment of a parliamentary committee to ward off other unorthodox assaults by considering carefully all proposals designed for the "better Propagation of the Gospel." In a short time the gospel committee became the center of a heated controversy in which Owen and his associates again figured. For, in their zeal to advance their form of church polity, these ministers had submitted fifteen proposals to the committee, the two most important of which were for the establishment of a state church under Independent control and for partial toleration. How partial this toleration was to be was seen in various proposals, one of which had the various sects either agreeing to certain principles of Christianity or else not being allowed to hold their own services. Another provision stipulated that dissenters could attend Sabbath services either in the established church or in their own churches, with their location made known to the magistrates. Still another clause had the ministers of the state church being paid by the customary tithes, to which all people were expected to contribute regardless of their religious affiliations.[20]

Once these proposals were made public, the sects mounted vigorous opposition; for, in addition to the above restrictions, not one of the proposals maintained the idea of religious freedom as a basic human right. Furthermore, the enforced payment of tithes angered the militant liberals surrounding Vane, including Williams, who saw in these collections the continuance of the financial prop on which an established church rested. For them no real liberty of conscience could obtain until these hated payments were abolished and the idea of a state church completely refuted. Hence, among the many pamphlets and petitions sent the gospel committee in early March to protest Owen's proposals were a series of four papers by Major Butler. An officer in Cromwell's army and a dedicated tolerationist, Butler was opposed to any kind of an established church, a view shared by Williams, who published on March 30 *The Fourth Paper Presented by Major*

*Butler,* a twenty-seven-page pamphlet supporting Butler's views in behalf of religious liberty.[21]

In a short letter meant for the gospel committee, Williams indicated that these committee members were completely mistaken if they thought there was any single way of propagating the teachings of Christ to which all men would "agree in one unanimous Consent and Vote" (121). Both Parliament and the committee were therefore bidden to become aware of their inadequacies and to realize that many nations were still being fooled in regard to "the Piety and Equity of Soul freedom." Aware too of the pressure being put on Cromwell to back the establishment of the state church proposed by the Independents, Williams made use of a statement attributed to the Puritan leader to the effect that "he had rather that Mahumetanism were permitted amongst us, then that one of God's Children should be persecuted."

In his explanatory testimony Williams took positions similar to those Butler had taken on the nature of the ministry, the disposition of heretics, and the abstention of the civil arm in matters of conscience. While not opposed to both the ministers who had been "sent" forth by Jesus to preach and to the prophets stirred by the spirit of Christ during the period of the Antichrist, he was still disenchanted with those ministers who were to be licensed by the state, and who would probably haggle over what they were to be paid. Williams doubted that ministers such as these had ever been "sent," even though "all the Civil Powers in the World should submit to their Commissions and Sendings" (132). As for the proposal forbidding dissenters from holding services whose doctrines were not in accord with the basic principles of Christianity, Williams was in complete disagreement. To exclude false teachers and heretics was wrong since it was God's will that Christians and pagans, "the Wheat and the Tares . . . be permitted to die in the common Field of the World together" (132).

It was toward "the state's power in spirituals," however, that Williams pointed his strongest thrusts against the establishment of a national church. Magistrates had no right to go outside their immediate sphere of duty, since it was obvious in recent years that "God hath made it evident that all Civil Magistracie in the World is merely and essentially Civil" (133). As for the claim of the Anglican clergy that Henry VIII's title of spiritual head of the

English church had been prepared for by "the Jus Divinum" of the authority of princes in spirituals as worked out by the Hebrew kings, Williams had no sympathy. For him Jesus was the antitype of the Hebrew monarchs, thus nullifying their effect on all monarchs in human history. Furthermore, any claim of the temporal ruler to supremacy in both the secular and religious realms was doomed on the basis of England's representative government where "Princes could not receive but what the Parliaments gave them, and the Parliaments could not give them but what the people gave the Parliament their Representative; which could not possibly be a Spiritual and Soul-power" (134).

The right of civil rulers to interfere in religious matters effectively negated, Williams proceeded then to clarify his position against an established church. To him such an institution came into being and became the focal point of those religionists who were absolutely certain that they alone possessed the one true faith, and who consequently sought the help of the magistrate to establish their church. Referring to the religious strife that had embroiled England on this score during the past one hundred years, Williams pointed out that the Catholics with their Latin mass had in turn been succeeded by the Protestants and their Book of Common Prayer, who in their turn had been replaced by the Presbyterians and their "Scotch Directories." And now in the saddle and seeking to rule the religious life of the nation were the Independents, whose efforts to institute their own version of a partially controlled church would not be much different from that of the Presbyterians. Certainly the role of a national church as Williams described it would help the present lawmakers to avoid the rocks that had led their predecessors to "woful shipwrack."

But, even if the Independents were to succeed in instituting their regimen on the nation, Williams was not unduly concerned, since it was simply a matter of time, he believed, before such "State-plants" would be plucked up by Jesus in order for religion "to work freely and in his own way" (134–35). In a passionate peroration, characteristic of him when he became deeply involved in defending his views, Williams urged Parliament to make up for the failure of their predecessors in office: here and now they had the opportunity to grant their people "absolute Soul-Freedom . . . so that, no person be forced to pray or pay, otherwise then as his Soul believeth and consenteth" (135).

In pleading against a hireling ministry, against the maltreatment of heretics, and against the intervention of magistrates in spirituals, Williams was expressing views which were in vogue for men of his stamp in the religious climate of 1652. However, in his insistence that Jews be extended their civil rights, Williams was introducing a comparatively novel idea into the religious controversies of the day (136). The Jews had long been denied admission into England, and those who had resided there since the Middle Ages had suffered great persecution at the hands of their Christian neighbors. And since their conversion had long been the objective of these same neighbors. Williams thought the action of insuring these long-suffering people the right "to live freely and peaceably amongst us," would do much to redress the harsh cruelties they had endured and hasten their Christianization. With the aid of Vane and his liberally oriented friends, he was successful in influencing Cromwell to remove a few of the immigration barriers that had previously excluded this minority group; thereafter they were allowed to enter England through the back door, so to speak. Simultaneously, Jews had begun to receive fair and equitable treatment in Rhode Island once they had started arriving there in the 1650's.

With the passage by the gospel committee of the Independents' first three proposals permitting magisterial intervention in spirituals, the primary purpose for *The Fourth Paper Presented by Major Butler* ostensibly failed. Moreover, the overthrow of the rump in April, 1653, closed any further Parliamentary consideration of the subject. But in April, 1652, Williams was much too busy writing other pamphlets bearing on the same subject to worry about the final disposition of any one of his tracts.

## II  The Hireling Ministry None of Christs

Written in April, 1652, just a few weeks after *The Fourth Paper Presented by Major Butler*, when it was apparent that Parliament was not yet prepared to forgo the collection of tithes, *The Hireling Ministry None of Christ*[22] was a second appeal to the lawmakers to reconsider their stand. From the question of an established church and its state-supported clergy, actually the sole point at issue, Williams, with his usual skill, lifted the whole matter into the larger realm where the civil government was enjoined to allow the people "to choose and maintain what Worship and Ministry their Soules and Consciences are perswaded of." This idea, however, was not fully insisted upon until he first laid bare the deleterious results both to the state and the people of a "hireling ministry."

Like Milton, who had in *Lycidas* already criticized the motives of those preachers who "for their bellies' sake,/Creep and intrude and climb into the fold," Williams found the primary interest of the hirelings to be "for fatter and rancker Pastures." What disturbed him even more was the whole attitude of expedience that motivated these men to doff their ecclesiastical affiliations and to switch from Catholicism to Protestantism and, once within the latter faith, from Anglicanism to Presbyterianism and finally to Independency (152–53). These quick shifts were attributed to a number of reasons, all of which afforded Williams an opportunity to condemn everything relevant to an established church.

The preface indicated once more his "humbly bold" and eager desire to argue his ideas with anyone so inclined. A particularly illuminating passage disclosed the fullness of experience on which he based his confidence: "I have not been altogether a stranger to the Learning of the Aegyptians, and have trod the hopefullest paths to Worldly preferments, which for Christ's sake I have forsaken since I know what it is to Study, to Preach, to be an Elder, to be applauded; and yet also what it is also to tug at the Oar, to dig with the Spade, and Plow, and to labour and travel day and night amongst English, amongst Barbarians . . ." (153).

His various occupations having served no deterrent to his own ministerial activities, Williams consequently felt free to advise those truly dedicated spirits who had a calling for the pulpit to avoid coming "under the slavery . . . of a mercenary and Hireling Ministry." They were urged instead to enter other vocations rather than "cease from Prophesying." And Williams also anticipated certain legitimate queries that disputants might raise, particularly on the idea of soul freedom. For those inquiring whether Papists, Jews, and Turks could be expected to live in Protestant countries and hold their own religious services without fear, the answer was *yes*. This point he had made absolutely clear, he hoped, in his "late unwashing of M. Cotton's washing of the Bloody Tenent," where he had written that no opinion was "so bloody or so blasphemous" as that which did not allow to live "in a civil way of Cohabitation, the consciences and worships, both of Jewes and Gentiles" (155).

Among the ten "Particulars" Williams listed for discussion were the usual staples of his thought in regard to soul liberty and a state church, in addition to one dealing with the interruption and discontinuance of the apostolic succession, a subject which he had hitherto barely discussed (149-50). With the figure of Jesus taken to represent the White Troopers set forth in the early chapters of Revelation, the overwhelming of these same troopers in chapters six through nineteen symbolized the total rout of Christ Jesus' ministry and church "put to flight and retired into the Wildernesse of Desolation." This desolation was equated with the period of "the beast Antichrist," which, begun with Constantine, was continued by succeeding Roman Emperors and finally by the Popes, all of whom were manifestations of the selfsame beast, who to counteract God had stirred up his own witnesses and prophets to fight against.

These doughty stalwarts, including such protagonists as Wycliffe, Hus, Luther, and especially Calvin had wandered, however, "from the first Patternes and Institutions" of the Master (158, 161). These departures from Christ's "patternes" and his own experience had consequently not convinced Williams "that either the Begetting Ministry of the Apostles or Messengers to the Nations, or the Feeding and Nourishing Ministry of Pastors and Teachers, according to the first Institution of the Lord Jesus, are yet restored and extant" (160).

In light of this explanation Williams' temporary alignment with the Baptists in 1639 can be understood. Doubting the validity of his early baptism, Williams had joined the Baptists and had been rebaptized. But he soon left this group, not because he had begun to doubt the impropriety of his second baptism,[23] but because he had become convinced that no ministry on earth could trace itself back in a direct line to the apostles. This belief set him at variance with the Nonseparatist Congregationalists, for while agreeing with them that the office "derived chiefly from Christ," [24] he still felt this authorization derived from the apostolic succession, a status which in fact meant ordination; and a minister was no more qualified to administer before being ordained than "a husband

[to] enjoy his spouse before marriage." [25] To Cotton, though, it was not "Ordination . . . which giveth essence to the Ministers Calling, but the peoples choice." [26]

Another query Williams anticipated referred to the performance of the latter-day ministry as against the one God had raised up in the struggle against the Antichrist. It was in "their Gifts, their Calling, their Works, their Wages" that he found modern ministers to be most deficient. For even though the ministry at present pretended "to the Apostles Commission" to justify their calling, they, according to Williams never laid claim to the gifts manifested by the apostles. Nor had they solved the matter of the laying on of hands and the doctrine of Baptism, "the two Foundations of the Christian Religion." As for some ministers who claimed their authorization from the Church of England, and for others who said their authority derived from the people, Williams was not at all satisfied "that either, Christs succession did run in an Antichristian line, or that two or three godly persons might first make them selves a church, & then make their Ministers, without a preceding Ministry from Christ Jesus unto them, to gather, and to guide them in such their Administrations." [27]

That "Christs succession" could not proceed along antichristian lines was premised on a simple fact: by virtue of his being the Son of God, Christ could not have anything to do with a force so antithetical to his nature as the Antichrist. Again, Williams' opposition to a church's coming into existence by the gathering together of a few godly persons for that purpose, was particularly aimed against the Baptists who had probably influenced his thinking; for agreeing with him that the apostolic succession had ceased with the advent of the Antichrist, the Baptists insisted instead upon a spiritual succession, where persons filled with the holy spirit could join with others similarly inspired to establish their own places of worship. But to Williams there first had to be "a preceding Ministry from Christ Jesus" before a church could be formed. Thus to both the Congregationalists' and the Baptists' views of a truly authorized ministry, Williams was directly opposed.

In their works, also, the latter-day ministers were found to be deficient, since their ministrations were carried on "for the converting of a converted people." Yet in his day, Jesus had sent out his apostles to preach to the people first, after which the latter had become converted. And with Williams' sense of this same twofold ministry, one to go out solely to convert their auditors to Christianity, with the second group to preach to those so converted, his query was that "if we grant all Protestant Nations to be Christians, and so act with them in prayers as Christians, and the children of God; how can we pretend to convert the converted, and to preach unto them to convert them? One or other must be denied, to wit, that they are converted, or if unconverted, that we may offer up Christian and Spirituall Sacrifices with them" (163).

In the matter of wages, too, there was a vast difference between those who preached because they were filled with the spirit, and those who made "a Trade of Preaching" and who, when not paid, would "no longer pray." Thus the fruitage of the hirelings in awakening souls was found to be minimal in contrast to those inwardly called to preach like one Samuel How, a cobbler, who without benefit of humane learning had become an excellent "Scripture learned man." How in fact served as an example of the "Mechanick" preachers whom Williams believed had more of the spirit of devotion and of the ministry than did the hirelings, who were either Oxford or Cambridge graduates (167). Not that Williams meant to downgrade collegiate studies or the language training offered at both universities; still their respective curriculums left much to be desired when compared with a truly fervent desire "to suffer for the name of the Son of God."

Williams' stand for a devout ministry based on spiritual worth alone was of course in direct contrast with that held by the Bay elect; the latter sought in the union of the religious and the worldly, of the spiritual and the secular, of the Bible and "humane learning" the bases for the learned clergies of elders to whom congregations would have to submit because of their inferior education. Accordingly, Williams advanced several reasons why certain practices at Cambridge and Oxford, when compared to Jesus' last will and testament, were "found to be none of Christs," the status which conservative Puritans wished them accorded.

For example, the universities' appropriation of the term "Scholar," while relevant as applied to humane learning, completely annulled the biblical connotation of the word and its reference to anyone who was a believer and a saint. Again, the monkish and idle way of life led by the trainees for the pulpit came off second best when compared to the hardships endured by the apostles in their vocations as fishermen and tentmakers. "Popish and vaunting Titles" such as Bachelor of Divinity were also condemned as being completely opposed to Jesus' command, as were the childish ceremonies engaged in by the trainees whose showy religious apparel was also censured (169–70). Because of these deficiencies and the overweening sense of their own importance, Williams questioned whether the universities were indeed "the only Masters and Teachers of Religion and godlinesse, and all this in the way of the Hireling . . ." (172–73).

Still, were one to question where ministers were to derive from if not from "the seed-plots and Seminaries, the Universities," Williams' answer was simple. It was the government's responsibility to guarantee freedom of conscience to all sects and also to encourage the supply of "such true Voluntiers" who would give themselves wholly to the ministry because spiritually they could not do otherwise. Like Paul, these "voluntiers" would do any kind of work rather than see the ministry neglected; for their pay they would depend upon their auditors (183).

Yet the payment of ministers by tithes or by voluntary gifts was of small import in view of the tremendous changes Williams envisioned in a world where established churches would in time be a thing of the past. For, in his description of the mourning to be engaged in by the witnesses raised up by God during the period of the Antichrist, he outlined his version of the second coming of Christ, an event then considered imminent by most Puritans.[28] But before the millennium could be ushered in, the Papacy had first to be overthrown, an occurrence which would take the lives of vast numbers of witnesses as foretold in Revelation 11.[29] With these momentous events regarded as near at hand, Williams' failure to work more earnestly at converting the Narragansetts is better understood. To him, there was little reason for concern about the redemption of the North American natives when "we have Indians at home, Indians in Cornewall, Indians in Wales, Indians in Ireland, yea as to the point of true Conversion, and Regeneration by Gods spirit, who can deny but that the body of this and of all other Protestant Nations as well as Papish are unconverted. . . ."[30]

Going forth to convert without a powerful call or without the gifts that characterized Jesus' first ministry resulted, Williams admitted, in having "no faith [himself] to act, nor in the Actings and Ministrings of others."[31] In addition the time was not yet ripe for this work: the Antichrist had first to be destroyed. Like *The Fourth Paper Presented by Major Butler, The Hireling Ministry None of Christs* fell on deaf ears, for Parliament was not influenced to change its position on the collection of tithes.

### III  The Bloody Tenent Yet More Bloody

Written in Rhode Island and taken with him to England in 1651, *The Bloody Tenent Yet More Bloody* was a continuation of his feud with Cotton, which the latter had again taken up after having read Williams' *The Bloudy Tenent of Persecution.* Cotton, intent upon exonerating the Bay and himself from the onus of persecutors, which Williams had made them out to be, wrote two replies. The first, *A Reply to Mr. Williams his Examination,* once more related the episode leading to Williams' banishment and agreed with the magistrates' verdict of expulsion. The second, *The Bloudy Tenent Washed White in the Bloode of the Lambe,* a more extended tract and a chapter-by-chapter refutation of Williams' work, maintained Cotton's hardbitten conviction that persecution was entirely legitimate in the cases of those who sinned against fundamental points of religion. Both of Cotton's rejoinders were published in 1647, copies of which Williams soon read; and, as he put it, he was once more forced "to unwash Cotton's washings." This he proceeded to do for the next four years; the result was *The Bloody Tenent Yet More Bloody: By Mr. Cotton's endevour to wash it white in the Blood of the Lambe,*[32] the longest as well as the most important of the tracts Williams published in April, 1652, as part of his struggle for "the soul freedoms of the people." Essentially similar in content to its predecessor published in 1644, this second work is still important because of the increased strength of conviction eight additional years of mulling over his ideas on soul liberty had given him.

In three separate prefaces, addressed respectively to Parliament, to the general courts of Massachusetts, and to that most important of all audiences, the reader, Williams again reiterated political and religious ideas he had voiced in previous tracts. Again the point was made that Catholics should be allowed freedom of conscience if civilly obedient, and that Jesus had never signed over to civil magistrates the right to intervene in church disputes. The Long Parliament, while praised for having granted

toleration to the various sects, was bidden to realize the difference
between a state's granting of freedom of conscience to dissenters
and "the Equity and Piety [the natural right] of such a Freedom"
(6).

But the Bay and Cotton were of course the focus of Williams'
attack. And since the elect there had professed to come closer to
the teachings of Christ Jesus than had any other state, Williams
told their magistrates in no uncertain terms that they were persecutors "notwithstanding Mr. Cottons Vails and Pretences of not
persecuting men for consciences. . . ." Williams, after explaining
that he had not solicited the materials he had used in writing the
first *The Bloudy Tenent,* but that these had been "unexpectedly
and solemnly" sent him for his opinion, unabashedly proclaimed
the purpose of his present tract: to show up the doctrine of persecution "as one of the most Seditious, Destructive, Blasphemous
and Bloudiest in any or in all the Nations of the World . . ."
(26).

In his attack on Cotton, which carried over into the preface for
the reader, Williams meant to explode once and for all the myth of
his adversary's infallibility, a situation that had many people believing that God would not permit Cotton to err. This idolatry was
particularly abhorrent to Williams to whom all men were "but
Grass," with Cotton as fallible as anyone else (42–43). Nor did
Williams gloat over what he understood to be his foe's errors of
judgment on matters of conscience; he insisted instead that one of
the ways to Christ lay in allowing those whose worship differed
from the orthodox manner to go their way unmolested (48).

Holding a colloquy once again, Truth and Peace immediately
assailed Cotton for calling Williams unethical because the latter
had published Cotton's private letter to the Anabaptist eight years
previously. Instead, the action was seen as a constructive one in
having made known publicly the intolerance "Master Cotton pro-
claimeth on the House top" (54). Enjoying a far better sense of
protection and friendship in 1652 than in 1644—for Vane, Milton,
and Cromwell were sympathetic to the cause of soul freedom—
Williams was not at all disposed to hang back in his onslaught
against the man he felt to be most responsible for his banishment.
Thus the reason given behind Cotton's desire to substitute the
word *punishing* for *persecuting* was that the second term was "too

wilde and fierce an expression" to use as an explanation for the Bay's harsh actions toward nonconformists (57).

Cotton had a good reason in wishing to euphemize; for, even before Williams' second attempt at unwashing his foe's views, many English Independents, including John Owen, no great tolerationist himself, had written tracts taking vigorous issue with Cotton's *The Bloudy Tenent Washed White in the Bloode of the Lambe*.[33] Again, Clarke's recital of the harsh treatment accorded the Baptists in Lynn had caused Sir Richard Saltonstall, one of the Bay's old friends, to write Cotton that his spirit had been grieved by the sad things that "are reported daily of your tyranny and persecution in New England"; moreover, the practices of the New England magistrates had sullied their reputation and caused them to become "very low in the hearts of the saints."[34]

In answering the charge of persecution made against him, Cotton replied that individuals who declined membership with any of the New England churches served by their "Arrogance and impetuousness" to foment civil and church disturbances. Williams remembered only too well that this charge had been levied against him by the court in 1635, and that any doctrine inimical to the Bay version of church and state would be so assailed. Hence his counterassertion: the slandering of nonconformists as troublemakers and heretics was a favorite device all persecutors used to accuse those who disagreed with the official faith. Anyone, he claimed, had a right to refrain from church membership, and such declination did not have to be attended with any disturbance to the civil and religious orders.[35] If anything, the civil peace was most disturbed when those holding to the state faith endeavored to force others to their views. Furthermore, in claiming that dissenters were entitled to dispute against the orthodoxy and then simultaneously persecuting nonconformists, Cotton revealed once and for all that he believed his conscience alone to be "true and others false."

But persecution for "Arrogance and impetuousness" was for the Bay but one side of the coin; for excommunication of those who were already church members, but whose views were deemed heretical by their ministers, was also practiced. In either case, a person found guilty of disturbing the civil and church peace was automatically deprived of civil residence. To be not only spiritu-

ally punished, but also deprived of residence within the civil
realm, "the proper place for men as men to abide in," constituted
a twofold punishment Williams was certain Jesus never authorized (109). Moreover, the Bay's reliance on the text in Romans 13
as the basis for the use of the civil sword in church disputes was
predicated, to be sure, on the belief that magistrates were God's
ministers who were to do His work in religious matters. Once
again Williams made patent that, although the office of the magis-
tracy was of God, it was so in the same sense that marriage was,
"being an estate meerly civill and humane." And whatever power
these officers possessed derived solely from the people, who were
"the Original of all free Power and Government."

To support the legitimacy of civil intervention in religious matters, the Bay ministers had argued that, with the advent of Jesus,
only the national church of Israel had been abolished and that the
civil state was left intact and was to be governed by Moses' *Judi-
cialls* (321–22). This view thus made understandable the Congregational ministers' use of the civil arm whenever they thought
heresies and schisms were threatening the churches. For, according to Cotton, the churches were "integral and conservant causes
of the City," and any ecclesiastical eruption could be deemed
harmful to the welfare of the city (69). But, as already noted in
*The Bloudy Tenent,* Williams likened the churches or any religious groups in the community to private societies whose formation and dissolution were totally unrelated to the civil government, which was a totally secular institution. Still it was not the
Bay's confounding of the unrelated functions of church and state
that so deeply disturbed Williams; it was that the magistrates
called upon to intervene outside their civil sphere could hardly be
counted upon to be either godly or Christian, since "few wise or
noble" men were called to their position.

Cotton, in his effort to appear fair in his use of the civil arm to
suppress heterodox views, had insisted that magistrates not adequately informed on religious fundamentals were to desist, as it
were, from making decisions in this area until they were rightly
edified. But how many of these officials, Williams queried, would
admit their spiritual ignorance and testify they were not lawfully
invested in their office, but were "meer shadows . . . set on high
with empty names or titles only of Magistrate" (194). And since
Christian magistrates alone were of consequence in Cotton's

scheme of things, were the holders of this office to be thought of
as nonentities in the twenty-five parts of the world that had never
heard of "the sound of Christ Jesus"?

Earnest as Cotton might be in believing Christianity to be the
only true religion and all other faiths "not of God," he was reminded by Williams that these same pagans living outside the
limits of the Christian world believed as fervently as Cotton did in
"their lies of many Gods and Christs." Williams' awareness of and
interest in nations and peoples outside the normal ken of most
Puritans came, primarily, from his experiences with the New England Indians, his reading, and his knowledge of the Turks and the
Jews, which talks with his brother Sydrach and Cromwell had
afforded him. And what with Williams' wholehearted desire that
soul liberty be extended to all professing religionists, he consequently believed it to be impossible because of the world's many
disparate faiths for God to have ordained, as Cotton maintained,
that all peoples were to live under the Mosaic law "by one universal strictnes" (486).

In justifying persecution of those holding unorthodox views
Cotton claimed two solid results. First, oppression taught heretics
righteousness; and, second, Jesus' mandate was obeyed: to save
souls, bodies had to be destroyed (88, 256). For so believing, Cotton was viewed by Williams as being spiritually akin to those
churchmen, whether "Mahumetan, Popish and Pagan Priests,"
who, in espousing a state church and its one faith, were in effect
the greatest peace-breakers in the world. For to keep their positions, these churchmen had of necessity to stir up the magistrates,
the "Ministers Cane," to ward off those who, dissatisfied with the
official religion threatened the ministers' "profits, honours, and
bellies," which three factors, according to Williams, kept the Bay
ministers from granting freedom of worship to dissenters (175,
375).

As in *The Bloudy Tenent*, Williams again attacked the Bay position that peace and prosperity attended only those states in
which there was one official faith and cited Holland once more as
a country whose policy of toleration made possible such material
blessings as "Shipping, Trading, wealth, Greatnesse, Honour" (9).
As for those who feared Catholicism would spread if its adherents
were allowed to wordship freely, Williams, like Milton and Jefferson in their faith that ideas had to be tested in the market place,

was certain that the "free Conferrings, Disputings and Preachings of the Gospel of Truth" would be more than enough not only to convert Papists to Protestantism but also Jews, Turks, and pagans (316).

But any rapprochement or unity between the disparate groups just mentioned, let alone different factions within the Christian faith, was manifestly impossible at present. This fact was made clear in the appendix Williams attached to his tract addressed "To the Cleargie of the foure great Parties . . . namely, the Popish, Prelaticall, Presbyterian and Independent," in which he inserted ample evidence of the bitterness with which each group treated the others when each came into power. The English Independents were a current example of this fact; for, in addition to having removed thousands of Anglican and Presbyterian ministers from their livings, they now pursued a policy of restriction in which their countrymen were allowed the right to "walke at Liberty (to wit, within the Conjured Circle) so far as they please" (525). This restriction was apparently an allusion to the coercive policies inherent in the fifteen proposals set forth by the Independent ministers led by Owen. On the whole, however, the Independents did not take unkindly to Williams' strictures; for *The Bloody Tenent Yet More Bloody* was taken up "with applause and thanks by the army [and] by the Parliament." Parliament had in fact just begun to realize that there could be no resolution to religious strife "but by permitting of dissenting consciences to live amongst them." [36]

## IV   Experiments of Spiritual Life and Health

Published the same April that saw *The Bloody Tenent Yet More Bloody* put through the press, *Experiments of Spiritual Life and Health*[37] was the one composition least related to the controversies with which Williams was so concerned in the early spring of 1652. Because of the emphasis so frequently placed on his political ideas and on his colonizing activities, one tends to forget that Williams was first and foremost a deeply devout Calvinist, who was profoundly engrossed with his own salvation and that of others. Because of this spiritual concern, he wrote the *Experiments*, a long letter to his wife Mary, who, after having recovered from a serious illness, became discouraged over her spiritual state. Both *George Fox Digg'd Out of His Burrowes,* and the *Experiments* constitute the best insight into the day-by-day religious convictions Williams lived by; both works also afford the reader a deep view into the dour Calvinist theology by which the lives of all sincere Puritans were governed.

Williams actually meant the spiritual *experiences* one underwent and not experiments, as indicated in the title of the letter; for he cites the ways in which Mary, as well as other earnest Christians, could determine whether or not their souls were in a state of grace. Equally important, they were also shown how to keep themselves in this spiritually nourished condition despite assailing weaknesses and doubts.

On the whole, the devotional and evangelical tone of the *Experiments* was no different from that expressed in the countless seventeenth-century diaries that inquire into and record the nature of the devotional life. In spirit though, Williams' work was altogether different in that it set forth no formal check marks, so to speak, to determine whether one's heart was favorably disposed toward the things of the spirit. With such insignificant matters as whether God had been the last thought one entertained upon retiring, or whether one's mind strayed from paying strict attention to the Sunday sermon, Williams was not concerned. For him salvation lay in the depth and zeal with which the soul hungered for God and sought to obey His laws.

The dedicatory note to Lady Vane explained the circumstances under which this "private and sudden discourse" to Mary, his "poor Companion and Yoak-fellow," came to be penned (47–50). He had heard of her illness and recovery while negotiating and trading with the Indians from his post at Cocumcussot, where in the "very wild houses" of the savages he had managed to collect his thoughts to send off to Mary. Anxious lest his style might seem "to this refined Age too rude and barbarous," he soon showed whose commendation he sought: "And yet, is the Language plaine? it is the like Christs: Is the composure rude? such was his outward Beauty: Are the tryals (seemingly) too close? such is the two edged Sword of his most holy Spirit, which pierceth between the very Soul and Spirit, and bringeth every thought into the obedience of Christ Jesus" (48).

Having no idea when he wrote the letter of offering it to the public, he subsequently viewed its publication as an opportunity to sow "a little handfull of spiritual seed," a purpose that could best be fulfilled if his readers were alerted to an awareness in these "poor Experiments of those Personall excellencies" every devout believer possessed. The outline of its contents unfolded the threefold purpose he meant his letter to fulfill. First, those weak in faith were to be told that they could rejoice, since they were merely at the bottom rung of the spiritual ladder which they had to ascend to make true the beatitude that to the poor in spirit belonged the kingdom of heaven. Second, those strong in spirit were to be made even stronger in their religious strivings. Third, all believers were to be shown that, with the aid of God, a healthy spiritual life could be maintained (52–54).

Important in disclosing the religious convictions by which its author lived, *Experiments* is no less interesting for the light it sheds on the gentleness and solicitude of the husband and father for his wife and children. Because he was unable to visit them soon, he was taking the opportunity in the letter to send "an hand-full of flowers made up in a little Posey, for thy dear selfe, and our dear children," a gift he hoped would remain long after he had left this earth. The "little Posey" of course was the spiritual aids he had prepared in Indian wigwams for Mary to mull over, but her comprehension of these helps he was more than a little concerned about. For, though her spiritual inclinations were strong, he knew that her ability to read was limited (56).

Certain that her recent recuperation from a grave illness had been a forcible reminder that the "Candle of this vaine life" was soon blown out, he suggested that the duty of Christians lay, like trim and tight ships, in always being ready for God's "holy employments of us in the greatest tempests." And, if the outward man was subject to vicissitudes in matters of health, as Mary had recently experienced, so much more did the inner man need to be kept cheerful as men made their way through this world. For this purpose Mary was offered a series of ten "trialls and arguments," all of which emphasized a hunger for the things of the spirit. This craving was best epitomized in the last "triall," which stressed the sense of unhappiness one was to feel at the lack of Christliness in his life when compared to its presence in the lives of the martyrs (60–69). These Christlike inclinations he and others had seen in Mary, his "dear love and faithful companion"; his hope was that she had discerned these same tendencies in herself.

The practical nature of Williams' piety was readily seen in the advice Mary was given to express her spiritual qualities in relation to God, to her fellow man, and to herself—the Christian's three major relationships in this life. In all three connections the indispensable ingredient to be maintained was cheerfulness of disposition, an objective best attained by studying scriptural instances exemplifying this trait. If efforts in approximating in her own life the "heavenly patterns" set before her did not fully succeed, these failures were to serve as a "holy looking glasse to discover to us our soul spots" for the purpose of correcting them.

Whether one's inner man was rightly disposed to God could be ascertained in some twelve positive "arguments," all of them geared to the typical Puritan commitment of putting God first in all one's activities and of striving constantly to improve one's moral life in accord with the Mosaic Decalogue. Ever the Separatist, Williams cautioned those seeking to adhere to Christ's ordinances in all their purity to "separate from all false worships, Gods and Christ" (82). Having organized his letter as a sermon with its questions and answers, he anticipated the objection that hypocrites could claim that they manifested the same spiritual stirrings ascribed only to the devout. But, said Williams, the difference between a sincere and a deceitful Christian was that the insincere one would live no more righteously than "may serve his own turne." Moreover, there were various ways of detecting hypocrites who claimed their souls to be in a sound state of health vis-à-vis God, as compared to souls truly fervent and prayerful. The latter prayed privately, unceasingly, importunately for heavenly blessings; but the former loved to be seen of men when they prayed. And when their prayers for earthly things were not answered, they could be found running "to the Devill in evil means, murmurs and despair" (76).

In the soul's relationship to itself, the greatest weight was placed on the need for self-sacrifice and otherworldliness, with the latter condition meaning that this world and its comforts were to be used "as if we used it not." The best indication of the sound spiritual state of one's soul lay in its hatred and abhorrence of sin, an attitude of mind that served to disclose another difference between the worldly person and the true Christian. Already regenerate, the latter could fight sin as an element totally foreign to his heavenly nature; and the worldly or unregenerate person could neither avoid sin nor its appearance because it was "his nature and Element." All he could really hate were the damaging and disgraceful effects wrought by it (91).

As would be expected, Williams gave the highest priority to doing the right thing by one's fellow man; and such activity was regarded as the best way of glorifying God. Compassion and love for all mankind, whether or not people were of the household of faith; the ability to withstand the onslaught of sin; and readiness to surrender one's temporal life so dear had salvation become— these were some of the other qualities one was expected to develop in his dealings with others. Cited for their spiritual significance were Moses and Paul, whose lives furnished excellent examples of "the greatest strength, and health, and beautie of a Christian life."

Aware that his long letter might tire his wife's patience and cause her to stop reading it, Williams summarized the essence of his spiritual monitions: a believer always needed to wear Jesus' teachings around him very much like a cloak. Furthermore, the truly devout were to welcome constant spiritual purgation, since this cleansing was instrumental in "slaying and . . . purging . . . the filthy humours and corruptions of pride, securitie, uncleanness, self-love, covetousness, and what ever else remains behinde of the body of death in us" (104).

In ending his letter, Williams pointed out how the lack of true Christianity on the part of its adherents had throughout the ages constantly met with God's displeasure. Besides the usual wars, famines, and pestilences, which in the past had taken lives, were listed the evils of idolatry and false worships which signified an even greater loss: the souls of those engaged in these practices. Still if the afflictions he had just noted, including the biblical promise of the earth's destruction by fire, were not enough to make Mary become more spiritually vigorous, she was advised to think now and then of death and its terrible inevitability. This last fact understood, life would then appear as nothing more than a "vaine puffe," serving solely for "our purging and fitting for an eternall Glory" (113). Because of the priority given by Williams to the spiritual sense of things, it is difficult indeed to deduce that the political and the social aspects of this temporal life, however important, were for him more than transient concerns. Life eternal was his goal; everything else in the temporal scheme of things was subservient to that quest.

## V The Examiner Defended

In the spate of anonymous controversial tracts that spewed forth in 1652 apropos of the establishment of a national church, three appeared in which the second and third, as was so characteristic of the period, were written as a result of their writers' agreement with or rejection of the views of a prior pamphlet, one in this instance entitled *Zeal Examined.* Espousing the cause of absolute religious freedom and probably written by Vane or someone with the same liberal inclinations, it was soon attacked by *The Examiner Examined,* which upheld the principle of a state church with its accompaniment of civil authority in spiritual concerns. To round out matters, in April appeared *The Examiner Defended,*[38] a defense of the views contained in *Zeal Examined.* Discovered as late as 1930, *The Examiner Defended,* because of its diction, content, and style, could have been written by no one but Williams, who probably undertook the task because Vane, or whoever had written the first tract, was either ill or away on official business (197). While adding nothing new to Williams' canon, the tract succinctly summarized his major ideas and, except for an ironic passage or two, was temperate in tone.

Twenty-two replies to a like number of questions propounded in *The Examiner Examined* constituted Williams' attack on his unknown adversary, whose entire argument revolved around two basic themes: that the civil magistrate or ruler occupied at present the same role of nursing father that the ancient Hebrew monarchs had exercised, and that idolatry was a vice not to be tolerated at any cost. In his answer Williams ascribed the many changes of faith and the consequent turmoils that England had suffered since the reign of Henry VIII to the "decree of Heaven . . . to break to pieces the more than iron Yokes and chains upon the souls and consciences of men" (205). He disagreed, therefore, with his adversary's contention that the spiritual growth of the nation would be hastened by holding the "true worship and service" that a state church would necessarily institute because of the ruler's thoughtful desire to benefit his subjects.

For Williams, experience on this score had shown otherwise: "true worship and service," which was always helped along by the civil sword, was always accompanied by hypocrisy on the part of those so coerced (218). And, while the monarchs of Israel served as nursing fathers because of the peculiar relationship of the Hebrews to their God, the office of the civil magistrate at this time was "meerly and essentially Civill," with his powers delegated by the people in whom lay "all Authority and Rule." Hence it was inconceivable that the citizenry in their natural capacities would turn over any religious power to their rulers (210). Thus any monarchs who forced their subjects to any particular mode of worship were engaged in nothing more than "a soul-rape and tyranny." To think otherwise, one had merely to consider what happened when this coercion was resisted: a recent casualty of the nursing father concept was the late Charles I, whose downfall was ascribed to his desire to impose Laud's episcopacy upon the Scotch Presbyterians (213).

His indictment against a state church well begun, Williams went on to show that the saving food—the correct doctrine a monarch was to provide for the enlightenment of his subjects—presumed the authorization of a national church; but this was an institution that Jesus had never sanctioned. He also attacked the idea that the coercion of dissenters was necessary in order to insure the grace and consequently the prosperity of a nation; ample evidence existed that affluence was the lot of many lands that had never even heard of Christ (215).

Denying the magistrate the office of latter-day caretakers of their subjects constituted only one-half of Williams' indictment; the other half denied him the right to punish idolaters whether heretics or blasphemers, since the purpose of Christianity was not to destroy men's lives. If those who dealt harshly with idolaters examined their motives closely, they would find that at bottom their motivation was nothing but "a plain Merchandizing of the word of God." Included among the more notorious offenders in this regard were the hireling ministers who had turned the ministry into "a Trade and Living." Granting the premise that ministers had to be paid for their services, Williams still found far too many among them who would preach only for "so much or so much," a far cry from those early faithful Christian preachers, who when they found their spiritual efforts inadequately recompensed, worked manually for their maintenance (253–54). The payment of tithes, too, whereby the upkeep of these hirelings was assured, was seen as an oppression of nonconformists which in time would deprive England of her prosperity (218).

All told, the pursuit and ultimate destruction of idolaters which an established church would insure was viewed as being the practice in all ages of "not tolerating . . . of Christ Jesus" or any of his followers. One had merely to look at the present age to find this practice still followed by Catholics, Anglicans, Presbyterians, and Independents, who, in their mistaken zeal that theirs alone was the true faith, would have "no people . . . live but Christians" (204). Yet, despite the efforts of the above four groups to establish a state church, such an institution evidently was not to be for the English nation, since the Solemn League and Covenant, enacted in 1644 for this purpose, had not been implemented (265–66).

Williams had yet a few words to say on what he believed constituted the basic elements of a true faith. For him, of course, Christianity as practiced by Christ Jesus was the only true religion; but believers were free to seek whatever faith they desired. In this quest they would find "Natural corrupted Reason" a help in gaining a conviction of the existence of God; reason alone, however, would not be enough to ensure their salvation. For this, the light of revelation was necessary, which could be bestowed by God alone (242). Moreover, this lack of light and dependence on reason alone, Williams viewed as the basis of the many "monstrous opinions" men entertained about God and of the foolish and "ridiculous kindes and waies of worship" to which they subjected themselves.

But that this revelation was possible for all men was answered in his discussion of his adversary's query on whether certain doctrines necessary for salvation should be called "Forms." To Williams, all religions were bound up in forms, "Forms of Confessions, Forms of Prayers, Formes of Churches, Formes of Worship," but these alone could not remove the ills of the established churches that had come into being with the Apostasy." For even had a synod under the auspices of Jesus worked out a uniform code of forms covering every aspect of church life, there was still nothing in the Master's teachings for their implementation by force. Religious convictions were to be gained only as men searched and questioned the basic texts of their respective faiths:

"What reason of Christianity, or Civility, that the Talmud of the Jewes, the Alcaron of the Turks, and the Canons of all sorts of Popes must not be questioned?" (273).

On this basis of asking all sincere religionists to dig deeply into the fundamental premises of their respective faiths, Williams ended his attack on *The Examiner Examined*. This admonition to probe also made understandable his query as to the kind of Christianity that would not permit the formation of churches, the appointment of ministers, and the teaching of doctrines "but what the Civil Sword shall say is true and Orthodox?" (273–74).

CHAPTER 5

# Altercation with the Quakers

FOR no other of his actions has Williams been so severely criticized as for his denunciation late in life of the Quakers and their doctrines. For in his indictment in *George Fox Digg'd Out of His Burrowes*[1] of a greatly harassed sect, the apostle of soul liberty was accused of having renounced the fundamental religious principle by which Rhode Island had been settled and which had been so eloquently expressed in *The Bloudy Tenent*. But no statement can be further from the truth. To be sure, modern historians, following the tack of Parrington and James Ernst, who, having portrayed the Rhode Islander as a political and social liberal, were at a loss to explain his condemnation of Quakerism except as a glaring error of judgment which took place in the long winter of his retirement. A careful study of Williams' earlier writings, however, would have made clear to these scholars that nothing so completely dominated Williams' thinking as his religious sense, and that in this respect, he was nothing more than an illiberal and staunch Calvinist to whom the Bible was primary in all matters of faith and practice. That the Society of Friends, as the Quakers were first called, downgraded the Scriptures in this respect was one important reason Williams scorned their basic tenets.

A thoughtful examination of Williams' written works discloses that he never held back in harshly rebuking any religious groups, let alone the Quakers, when he thought they deserved censure. Hence, once convinced that the Papists represented the Antichrist, they were evermore for him the whore of Babylon and the corruptor of all true religion. And in the above sense he lashed out constantly at Papist practices whenever he found them akin to those of the Quakers. Himself utterly convinced that Protestantism of the Separatist type was the only true faith, a fact he was sure would reveal itself by reason and discussion, he still attacked

the Bay Nonseparatists for playing both sides of the religious
street, so to speak. Moreover, his short affiliation with the Baptists
terminated when he had qualms about the authority behind his
second baptism.

Still no sect, however unorthodox their beliefs, suffered Williams' wrath as vehemently as did "the cursed sect," as he termed
the Quakers; and, in his diatribe against them, he admitted he had
"used some sharp Scripture language." Altogether, his highly
scathing and vituperative arraignment of their beliefs is in contrast to the tone of moderation which characterized his controversies with Cotton. But to understand the reason behind this harsh
attitude, one must remember that the Society of Friends under
the leadership of George Fox was but one of the numerous noisy
and ranting sects that had emerged as a result of the Puritan victory over Charles. They were not in the third quarter of the seventeenth century the sober group of humanitarians they since have
become; in Williams' day they were a fanatical, unruly group who
shocked the sober citizenry by the antics of both their male and
female adherents who thought nothing, for instance, of running
naked through the streets to proclaim their beliefs.[2]

As we have already seen, as president of the colony from
1654–57, Williams was forced to threaten several Quakers with
legal action for their refusal to bear arms for the colony's defense.
He soon became so irritated with their incivilities that he went so
far as to urge legal enactments against them for their failure to
remove their hats before officials.[3] But these incivilities were
merely irritations; it was their unwonted enthusiasm and bizarre
claims to have won their eternal salvation instantaneously, so to
speak, as well as their failure to hold to the rationalistic premises
Williams thought necessary to any discussion of theology that
earned them his contempt. To one as energetic as he had been in
his earlier days, their sitting quietly at prayer meetings until they
felt the monitions of the spirit was utterly incomprehensible; and
this waiting for the moment of truth he termed the "worship [of]
a dumb Devil."

Ironically enough, what Quakerism at bottom based itself upon
was not an altogether unexpected offshoot of basic Puritan convictions. For, in following Luther's dictum prescribing no need for an
intermediary in the individual's relationship to God, the Puritans
gave their imprimatur to the claim that each individual was his

own best guide in matters of conscience. In actual practice, however, these same Puritans first of all laid stress on a learned clergy, whose pious but erudite sermons derived from biblical texts were fashioned for the avowed purpose of guiding submissive congregations, albeit those of the elect. To the Quakers, on the other hand, such externals as an educated ministry and scholarly sermons were unnecessary; all that believers had to do was to put their faith in the inner light, "which lighteth every man that cometh into the world."

That Williams was ever true to his conviction that any sect could find a haven in his colony free from religious interference as long as its members obeyed the civil laws was seen in his stand, together with that of his fellow colonists, against the United Colonies who sought to have the Quakers excluded from Rhode Island where they had fled to escape Bay persecution. In their reply to the Bay, asserting that "freedom of different consciences" was the basis of their charter, and that they had "no law . . . to punish" any who expressed their religious views solely by words, the Rhode Islanders still made it clear that Quakers found disobeying civil enactments would be punished.[4]

For Williams there were, however, other factors to be considered besides disobedience to duly constituted law. Having first become acquainted with the Society of Friends during his second sojourn in England, he had become accustomed to their "lying Quakings and Tremblings" and to their insistence that "there were no sins in them." For him, this assertion signified an arrogant sense of self-righteousness that made them believe they were the sole possessors of the only assured means of the salvation of the individual soul. Upon his return to Providence, he proceeded to study the works of their more noted writers, including those of Fox, whose important work *The Great Mystery of the Great Whore* (1659), he found "poor . . . lame, and naked"—devoid of solid worth.

But not until 1672, or almost two decades after the Quakers had first arrived in the colony, did his irritation with them come to a head. So numerous were they by this time that they had won control of the colonial government, and one of their actions had been to free William Harris from jail, where he had been awaiting trial on charges of treason to the colony. To be sure, Harris may have gained his release because of his prior conversion to Quakerism, an action Williams viewed as consistent with Harris' desire to promote his commercial endeavors by trading with them.[5]

What finally galvanized Williams into action was Fox's triumphant tour through Rhode Island in the summer of 1672 amidst the tumultuous acclaim of his fellow Quakers. Lame with the infirmities resulting from a lifetime of hard work, Williams was still infused, however, with the fighting spirit which in 1645 had caused him to write *The Bloudy Tenent*. Now nearly thirty years later, he was to defend his soul's beliefs in public for the last time, and, in anticipation of Fox's tour, he reread *The Great Mystery of the Great Whore*. This time he found Fox's arguments "so weak and silly, so Anti-Christian and Blasphemous" that he felt impelled to challenge the Quaker leader to a debate on the validity of his creed.

An incident during the previous year had probably confirmed his desire for a public discussion. In order to present his Calvinistic views, he had at that time gone to Newport where the Quakers were having their annual assembly. As he tried to get across to them "some Considerations about the True Christ and the false," he found himself suddenly cut off by interruptions in the form of prayers and singing, with the meeting soon terminated. This unhappy incident resolved him "to offer a fair and full Dispute" by taking advantage of a suggestion to this effect made by Edward Burrough, one of Fox's most ardent disciples, in his epistle in his leader's book.[6] This resolve to debate with Fox may have been the reason Williams did not go to meet the "most deified" Fox when the latter toured Providence.

Williams issued his challenge in the form of fourteen Propositions which he inserted in a letter which he gave to Captain John Cranston, deputy governor of Rhode Island, to be forwarded to Fox then at Newport. But because Cranston, a Quaker himself, let a fellow Quaker know of the challenge, the letter dispatched on July 15 did not reach its destination until eleven days later, when Fox had already departed for England. Because of these circumstances, Williams would not believe that Fox had not received his message, but felt that the latter had actually made a "run for it" at the advice of "the junto of Foxians at Newport," who had decided that it was inadvisable for their leader at that particular time to hold forth publicly with the founder of Rhode Island (6).

Still, if Fox was unavailable, three able Quaker preachers, John

Burnyeat, John Stubbs, and William Edmondson were ready, and agreed with Williams' choice of towns for the debate to be held in. Accordingly, the first seven propositions were to be aired at Newport, with Providence selected as the site for the remaining seven. With August 9 set for the initial debate, Williams arrived at Newport the previous midnight, having rowed "with [his] old bones" the thirty miles from Providence.

The next morning the old Quaker meeting house was filled with supporters for both sides, including Baptists and Gortonists who had come to lend Williams their moral backing. Pitted against them were the many Quakers whose more prominent members, besides deputy governor Cranston and Harris, numbered Governor Easton and William Coddington, the latter having been converted to the doctrine of the inner light as early as 1665. Among the prominent Gortonists supporting Williams were Gorton himself and two of his most devoted followers, John Greene and Randall Holden.

The first day was taken up entirely with Williams' presentation of his first proposition, to the effect that the Quakers were not true Christians according to the Holy Scriptures (41). Using Fox's book from which he read passages, Williams was prepared to argue in the Cambridge manner of fully presenting his own views and then of allowing his adversaries the opportunity for rebuttal. But, if he expected his opponents to remain quiet until he had finished, he was due for a rude shock. He had, in fact, thought of having a moderator, but had given up the idea because of the "strange assurance" that, by exercising moderation and patience, his adversaries would also practice these same qualities.

But not having obtained a promise from them beforehand that only one of them at a time would speak in rebuttal, he found himself frequently interrupted; and, much to their advantage, he was verbally pounced upon by all three simultaneously (38). In fact it was not so much a debate as a wrangle in which Williams' vituperative remarks so aroused the Quaker preachers that they felt impelled to interrupt. And with good reason, for Williams' propositions were not so much reasoned arguments as harsh indictments of Quaker doctrine. When Williams asserted, for example, that their quaking and trembling movements were about the most "horrid and monstrous actions and Gestures" he had ever seen, his opponents cited Scripture to the effect that men were to work out their salvation with fear and trembling (46). And so it went. Williams' charges and scriptural testimony to corroborate his indictments were met with countercharges and their relevant biblical attestations by his opponents, only two of whom he appreciated: Stubbs, who was "learned in Hebrew and the Greek," and Burnyeat, "A moderate Spirit." The third, Edmondson, sorely tried the septuagenarian's patience, being only "a bundle of Ignorance and Boisterousness" (38).

That the charges and countercharges were extremely exasperating was seen in the fact that, when Williams' testimony was not being seized upon by his foes, hindrances came from the floor where supporters for either side let themselves be heard. And, before the day was over, so hectic had the verbal scuffle become that Governor Easton, Cranston, and William Coddington, Quakers though they were, felt impelled to ask fair play for Williams. Robert Williams, Roger's younger brother, who had earlier migrated to Rhode Island, where he was a schoolmaster in Newport at the time, was one of those who interrupted to protest against the Quaker trio for "Insulting and domineering over" his older brother (58, 131, 108).

So tumultuous were the first day's proceedings that Williams did not have an opportunity to finish presenting his initial proposition. The second day, however, was devoted to his second charge: the Christ the Quakers professed was not the true Lord Jesus Christ (68). As on the previous day, the debate soon got out of hand; and, according to Williams, "a mutual Conference and natural Disputation" fell into "Popular Orations and Sermons" when at one point Stubbs and Edmondson felt impelled to deliver homilies to the audience. These interpolations in the midst of the debate were typical of the different mental avenues through which both sets of disputants broached their views. To Williams, God could not possibly have been the source of these interruptions: "For we all knew that the Spirit of God was most purely Rational, and a Spirit of pure Order, and did not prompt or move men to break Hedges and leap over one Ordinance into another" (99–100). Thus was stated Williams' view of the difference between Puritan rationalism and Quaker emotionalism.

Illiberal and shortsighted as Williams may have been in his view of the Quakers, the fact that he assailed his neighbors as he did affords a good insight into what was a characteristic aspect of the

Rhode Island mode of life. If his earliest publication, *A Key into the Language of America*, opened a door into the culture of the North American Indians, then *George Fox Digg'd Out of His Burrowes* may be said to have introduced later readers into the provincial yet exciting and noisy existence Rhode Islanders enjoyed in its first half century as a colony. In an area where the population consisted of the dregs of society, as the Bay orthodoxy termed them, in the sense that they were heretics, malcontents, or simply refugees from religious conformity; where each group was jealous to preserve its own characteristics; where settlers like William Arnold, William Harris, and William Coddington were typical examples of men solely engrossed in working for their own private gain as against the public good, it was only natural that fierce rivalries and hostilities should erupt when various groups found their own interests or beliefs vehemently attacked by others. Because of this freewheeling sense of things it was only natural for Williams to have received in return the hard-hitting invective he himself dished out. Hence it was normal that he be jeered at as an "old man, old man" or be thought drunk when on the second day he took his place unsteadily because of fatigue. That he had caught cold and that his rowing to Newport had worn him out—that these were the reasons for his unsteady gait did not matter to either his Quaker opponents or to their followers in the assembly who found his remarks offensive, and who were therefore willing to put the worst construction on his impeded physical activities.

That Williams knew the nature of the battle he had gotten into was seen when, after working out the rules for the third day's war of words, he disdained the shift of repairing to his bed, and instead decided to put his "old Carcase" back into the fray (104). Still there were few in Rhode Island in 1672 who would have wanted things to be different from what they were in this respect. It was far better to have the freedom to express one's views and receive in return the scorn and contumely of one's auditors than to suffer complete suppression of one's beliefs, as was the case in the rest of orthodox New England.

To insure the airing of Williams' five remaining proposals at Newport, the Quaker disputants agreed to a fifteen-minute limit for each one. Upon their completion, the scene then shifted to Providence, where on August 17, the same time limit obtaining for the remaining propositions, the debate mercifully ended. From the very start Williams had meant to keep a record of his controversy with the Quakers and had tried to get a shorthand reporter for this purpose. Failure to find one and the restrictions placed on his thought by the fifteen-minute limit on his last twelve charges caused him soon after the debate to set down his version along with other matters which the "quarter of an hour would not then permit." Published in Boston in 1676 as *George Fox Digg'd Out of His Burrowes,* the title itself a pun on the name of the famous pamphleteer, the bulky volume was his greatly amplified account of the entire debate. For his conventional Calvinistic stand, he was applauded by the same Bay orthodoxy, whose forebears, ironically enough, had wanted forty years previously to ship him back to England because of his Separatist views.

Thanks to Williams' retentive and accurate memory, none of the Quaker disputants questioned any factual statements made in his text. But his scornful tone, and his mockery of their doctrines and practices so infuriated them that Fox and Burnyeat replied to his diatribe in *A New England Fire-Brand Quenched,* published in 1678. For invective and raillery, the Quaker text far surpassed Williams' tract, which, to be sure, had provided his two adversaries with an excellent example.

Yet from the basis of Calvinism there were many reasons for him to have been contemptuous of Quaker doctrines. First, there was their scorn for the primacy of the Bible. Instead, Fox and his followers claimed this prerogative for the inner light, which they asserted to have existed "before the Scriptures, and gave forth Scriptures, and therefore was above the Scriptures and therefore is not judged or tried by the Scriptures, but they by it" (49). To Williams, on the other hand, there was no doubt that God had set forth His mind "in the old and new Scriptures or Writings" (63). To be sure, he realized that the God who had inspired the writing of the Scriptures existed prior to its composition; but, once written, the Bible served all Calvinists as the complete guidebook to the Christian experience; and, that without it, there was simply no understanding of Deity and of His means of salvation (454).

The Quakers did not completely discount the Scriptures; but, when they did consult the good book, they were accused of reading the latest English translation available, whereas it was only in the early Hebrew and Greek versions "in which it pleased the holy

Spirit of God first to write his mind and will unto us" (200). The early Christians, in fact, were in a far better position to understand these early accounts since they knew Hebrew, as well as Latin and Greek, "all which Helps the . . . Leaders of the Quakers want." Their failure to acknowledge the Holy Scripture as the "Declaration of the mind of God" Williams imputed to the Quaker refusal to forego "their pretences of Traditions and Revelations" by which the devil had ensnared them (203).

With the Quaker de-emphasis of the Bible went their downgrading of the role Jesus played in Christian history. For the Puritans, the Master Christian had been a living person, who after fulfilling his mission of establishing Christianity, had died in Jerusalem before returning to his Father. But for the Society of Friends, Jesus was to be found "in every mans heart that cometh into the world"; this equating of an everpresent Christ within everyone was in effect a repudiation of the Calvinistic understanding of a physical Jesus who had lived instead in a world of men. So insistent was Williams for a clear-cut answer on this issue, that the last question asked of his trio of opponents at Newport was where the Jesus mentioned in the Bible now resided. To their reply that Christ was now within, Williams' retort was "then must his Body be Ubiquitary . . . then must he have Infinite multitudes of Bodies" (213). Furthermore, in setting up "a voice or motion within" to displace the historical Jesus of the Scriptures, the Quakers were accused of denying the "visible Kingdome and Church and Institutions" that this same physical Jesus had introduced and had ordained to continue until his second coming. This last statement the Quakers countered with the assertion that the church was invisible because it was in God (101–2).

Their repudiation of the significance of the Bible and the historical Jesus were enough to earn them Williams' disgust; their claim, however, to the immediacy and infallibility of the inner light, and their insistence that they did nothing on their own volition "but [that] the immediate and infallible Spirit of God says and does all in them"—these last two assertions were certain to earn them his lasting scorn. For Williams, God worked only mediately in men's lives; and such activities as preaching, praying, reading, and conferring were the means whereby this mediation could be understood (127). As for their claim of infallibility, they were bidden to try the spirits, so easy was it for Satan to delude humankind. In the final analysis, Williams rested his case on pure rationalism; the source of all thoughts was to be determined by his "own Reason, or some Testimony of unquestionable Witnesses satisfying my Reason, or some heavenly inspired Scripture or Writing which my Reason tells me came from God" (127). To do otherwise was to forgo the experience and the wisdom humans had found valuable in their ascent out of darkness.

As for believing that everything the Quakers did or said was immediately inspired by the inner light, "the meanest Youth or Wench, if but a pretended Quaker," could accordingly surpass experts in all areas of human knowledge and activity (125–26). Arbitrary government, too, could eventuate from their claim to infallibility, since no written laws would be needed for the guidance of the community. And Quaker magistrates being infallible, of course, could not possibly err in their judgments, and thus would unwittingly turn persecutors, punishing all those not guided by the inner light (167).

The ease with which the Quakers promised mankind salvation was another sore point to their Calvinistic opponent. For example, all a drunkard had to do to be saved was to listen "to a Spirit within him, to say Thou and Thee, and think himself equal and above all his former Superiours. . . ." For Williams, salvation was an altogether different process. Because of the Puritan belief in man's total depravity, Williams insisted that sin be recognized as such, and "as greater than the greatest filthiness in the world." For him the weakness of the Quaker position lay in their inability to comprehend that the universe, both seen and unseen, could in no way be weighed in the same balance with "Gods most holy and inconceivable justice. . . ." At no other point in his writings did Williams bring to his readers the awesomeness of the doctrine of predestination than in his indictment of the Quakers for having embraced the Arminian concept of universal atonement and the eventual redemption of all mankind. Such salvation was utterly "contrary to the true Protestant Doctrine of a Certain Number of Gods Elect or Chosen drawn by mercy, out of the Lumpe of Lost Mankind according to Gods Appointment from Eternity, by his Call in Time, by his holy Word and Sprit" (208).

The Quaker claim that they were already as perfect as God in holiness as well as "in Power Omnipotent, Omnipresent, Omniscient," Williams refuted on two counts: first, the admonition given

Christians to grow in grace; and, second, the absoluteness of
Deity, who knew no human measures or degrees. Their claim to
perfection was in fact likened to Fox's starting to sew a shoe and
immediately boasting "that the Shoe is perfect." Still, it was not
merely the basis on which their faith rested that so deeply aroused
Williams; their daily actions and practices, as has been already
indicated, also elicited his contempt. Like Milton and most Puritans generally in his concept of women as a lesser creation of
Deity, Williams found the Quaker practice of sending out women
to preach not authorized by "Apostolical first Christian practice."
Again, such incivilities as their refusal to salute strangers and to
bow their knee to superiors was also held against them, as were
"their dumb and silent meetings," which were devoid "of Common
Humanity . . . or promise of Christ to such a worship." Also criticized was their lack of appreciation for music, an "Excellent . . .
gift of God," together with their cacophonous way "of Toning
and singing"; their practice of selling liquor to the Indians was
also condemned (33).

All told, the Quakers' "spiritual Pride" was "the Root and
Branch of [their] whole Religion," which Williams mentioned in
a letter he wrote "To the People Called Quakers," and which
served as one of the three prefaces to *George Fox Digg'd Out of
His Burrowes.*[7] Taken to task by the Quakers for not living in
church ordinances himself, Williams was forced to reveal the
depth of his Seeker position. For him it was one thing to repudiate
the visible kingdom of Christ Jesus, as the Quakers did with their
notion of an invisible kingdom; it was, however, an entirely different matter to be absolutely certain about the essential validity of
the many churches pretending "to be the true Christian army and
officers of Christ Jesus." If the members of these churches could
show him "after all my search and examinations and considerations" how the grace of God came to them—and it was his considered opinion that some of these churches came closer than others
"to the first primitive churches of Christ Jesus"—he would join
them.[8]

For the present, with his belief that no true church or ministry
had existed since the Apostasy, it was his duty to seek after this
pure institution and to await God's providence in this matter. As
to charges that Williams was unsettled in his beliefs, having been
in turn an Anglican, a Puritan, a Baptist, and finally a Seeker, the

statement is true; but for the wrong reason. Such was the intensity of his desire for a true church, for true forms, for a true ministry and worship, that no church as it was then constituted could fulfill these spiritual requirements. Far from having left all churches and religions, as he is often charged with, he was too sincere and devout a Christian to compromise his beliefs by joining any of the churches of his day after 1639, when he became disaffiliated from the Baptists. Quiet prayer meetings with other Seekers would have to suffice until the true church made its appearance on earth.

On the whole, his debate with the Quakers was a serious mistake. Nothing he said or published relevant to it added to his stature as a religious thinker. Deeply persuaded of the rightness of the basic tenets of Calvinism, he was unable to realize that the Quakers had a perfect right to hold to their convictions. And this attitude came from one who, in seeking after a literally pure church on earth, admitted in his polemics with Cotton that there was no one certain way of obtaining salvation. The only excuse that can be made for Williams is that his rationalism led him to drive out the intuitional aspect of faith. Unwise as was his decision to debate with the Quakers, his doing so revealed Williams' boldness and courage in uttering truth as he saw it.

## CHAPTER 6

# Williams' Significance for our Times

NO MAN fully transcends his own age. But from time to time a few, because of an inexorable and persistent throb in their characters, not only vividly express the ideological concerns of their day, but also advance and fight vehemently for concepts for which only posterity can properly thank them. It is in this sense then, that—as one looks carefully at a photograph of the International Monument of the Reformation at Geneva, Switzerland, where a statue of Williams is included along with those of such zealous religionists as Calvin and John Knox—one may inquire what this dour-visaged Calvinist could possibly have said and done three centuries ago that would be relevant to his fellow Americans of the Space Age.

As Victor Hugo so aptly observed, nothing is so powerful or irresistible as an idea whose time has come. And by the first third of the seventeenth century the moment was ripe, at least in England and in New England, for the clear and repeated enunciation of two ideas in the areas of government and religion, the gradual implementation of which in the Western hemisphere since that time have served as waymarks of rational and enlightened thought. By no means was Williams the originator of the ideas that church and state were distinct and separate spheres, and that one's religious beliefs were entirely one's own private concern. But it was he whom fate chose as one of the spokesmen and battlers for these concepts until they took hold at the outset of a new life in a new land, and in time became distinctive characteristics of what is termed "the American way of life."

The average American, so long used to the idea that his spiritual beliefs are his concern alone, cannot begin to appreciate the tremendous courage it must have taken for "loners" like Williams in 1635 to stand up to the Bay orthodoxy, and proclaim that civil magistrates had no right to punish offenses of a religious nature. To be sure, there were others—Anne Hutchinson and Samuel Gorton, to meniton just two—who also were heterodox enough to challenge Cotton and company, since the mental climate was ready for such defiance. However, it was Williams' insistence on absolute religious freedom and the wrath this brought upon him by the Bay that consequently paved the way for the founding of a haven for others similarly persecuted. Americans who have since enjoyed lives relatively free from religious persecution cannot begin to acknowledge their debt of gratitude to Williams until they have lived in or visited lands where separation of church and state is not yet established as a political and religious fact of life.

Any consideration, then, of Williams' importance for the highly technological and scientific nation America has become since the end of World War II must necessarily begin with an appreciation and understanding of this basic fact. Again in an age, thanks to computers and automation, where individuals feel they have been dehumanized to a number, and where our very great affluence has lulled many into a state of mind characteristic of Tennyson's lotos-eaters, much of modern dramatic literature and fiction, both here and abroad, has lent itself increasingly to exposing the supposed absurdity of contemporary life, with Kierkegaardian or Sartrean existentialism offered as the only viable philosophy by which per-plexed but thoughtful humans can endure the meaninglessness of their existence. To this state of affairs Williams would possibly suggest that at the root of modern man's feelings of purposeless-ness and alienation lay a lack of faith in an eternal God with whom he could feel a sense of kinship.

Nor does it matter that, by Williams' own admission he became converted to Puritanism at an early age and thereafter felt he was one of the elect in the scheme of predestination. Elect or not, for almost the last fifty years of his life he remained aloof from any church group, adhering tenaciously to his Seeker views which could find no church at that time in accord with them. And, far from finding life absurd, he made it his business to keep growing mentally and spiritually all because he, much like Walt Whitman, the greatest poet America has so far produced, had his foothold mortised and tenoned in the granite of eternity. And far from staining the white radiance of the latter, his years on this earth were to Williams a seed-time, so to speak, in which he simply could not accomplish enough or probe too deeply to reveal what this vital sense of existence meant to him.

For how else can one explain his multifaceted career which just on American soil had him engaged in a variety of activities, among whose more significant accomplishments saw a colony founded on the principles of political democracy and religious equality; a truce kept for a good many years between the Narragansetts and the United Colonies due in good part to his efforts at negotiation and mediation; and in England the publication of some seven or eight tracts espousing the idea of soul liberty, a principle whose basic validity is no longer questioned by Americans who have no religious ax to grind. And long after the Genets, Ionescos, the Becketts and other exponents of the absurd have passed into oblivion because of the essential barrenness of their credos, Williams will remain as one of the great affirmers of what Carlyle designated "the Everlasting Yea."

Nor must it be thought that, in working out his life-purpose, his religious thinking did not yield rich dividends for those of his fellow men who were ready to settle for the worldly sense of existence as sufficient for their needs. Political democracy, easily the most important contribution countries of the Western world have contributed to the art and practice of government, Williams early espoused; likewise religious liberty to all sects, including the Catholics, and this at a time when even those inclined like him toward soul liberty were not willing to grant this right either to the Papists or the Jews. Certain that his own life was caught up, as he put it, in the bundle of eternal life, he yet viewed the two just-mentioned principles as merely the necessary political and religious conditions whereby all individuals could best work out their present sense of existence.

Hence it is not as founder of a colony, where, in addition to religious freedom, the settlers were to govern themselves democratically, that is so important in an evaluation of Williams' significance for our day. To be sure, religious freedom he vehemently sponsored because, although sure of his own faith, he was certain, as he told Cotton, that the tenets of Calvinism did not hold for all of earth's inhabitants. Liberal as he was in this respect, he could still be the strait-laced bigot with the Quakers, whose theological principles he felt lacked a rational premise. And, ironically enough, the hope for political democracy that he envisioned for his colony was even in his lifetime eroded as the officials in the various towns succeeded in keeping the unallocated lands, the holding and possession of which were concomitant with suffrage, from going to latecomers to the colony. Yet for Williams a democratic form of government merely served as a base for his religious thinking, which needed that type of civil polity which simultaneously satisfied the political needs of its citizens, while providing the elect the necessary freedom to work out the problem of existence. Had the constitutional monarchy under Queen Victoria been in operation during his colonial days, he, one believes, would have gone along with it—so long as this mode of government satisfied its constituents and left them free in the religious realm.

So much then for his great concern in desiring a viable civil and religious climate so that all concerned could go their own secular and spiritual ways without hindering their neighbors from doing likewise. With this concern must be allied its necessary consequence: the inviolate right of every individual to his own private beliefs so long as these did not provoke civil disturbances. At a time when individual privacy is constantly being more and more invaded by private and public agencies, and when the cults of togetherness and conformity are very much seen and heard in the land, Williams would remind one of his essential preciousness in the sight of his Maker and of one's inalienable right to fight for the right of remaining the private person. Lest anyone think this to be an essentially selfish attitude, he should remember how ever ready Williams was to drop all private matters, even to the detriment of his family's welfare, to help bring about the public good.

Primarily unselfish, Williams came to this sense of generosity only after first having thought things out for himself in line with the principles of Christianity. Again, having out of his bitter experience bought truth dear, he would persuade men not to sell this commodity cheaply. Like Emerson, a later seeker for truth, Williams would have every individual trust himself and proceed in the direction of his dreams; and, like Thoreau, he would remind men, that if this destination partook of the nature of soul, no money was needed for the journey—only the courage of one's convictions. On this hard core of unselfish, rugged, and inspiring individualism would Williams rest his *raison d'être* for his time and ours.

# Notes and References

## Chapter One

1. *The Complete Writings of Roger Williams*, 7 vols. (New York, 1963). Hereafter to be cited as *Writings*, VII, 113.

2. Vernon Parrington, *Main Currents in American Thought* (New York, 1927), p. 66.

3. Emily Easton, *Roger Williams* (Cambridge, 1930); James Ernst, *Roger Williams* (New York, 1932); Samuel H. Brockunier, *Roger Williams* (New York, 1940); John Dos Passos, *The Ground We Stand On* (New York, 1941); Ola Elizabeth Winslow, *Master Roger Williams* (1957). All of the above follow more or less the line laid down by Parrington, with Ernst claiming that the cast of Williams' thought was "social rather than theological." See his *The Political Thought of Roger Williams* (Seattle, 1929), p. 205. Only Perry Miller in his *Roger Williams* (New York, 1953) disagreed with the Parrington thesis. As late as 1964, Robert C. Whittemore in his *Makers of the American Mind* (New York, 1964) wrote that "[Roger Williams'] importance in the history of the Holy Commonwealth as well as to posterity, is not so much religious as it is political."

4. "Wonderful" in the sense of the reverential fear caused by the death of Queen Elizabeth on March 24, 1603, and the alteration her death would bring to the lives of many of her subjects, many of whom had never lived under any other sovereign. See *Non-Dramatic Works of Thomas Dekker*, ed. by Alexander B. Grosart, 5 vols. (London, 1884), I, 86–87.

5. In a letter to Winthrop in 1632, he wrote he was "upwards of 30 than 25"; in a deposition in Town Clerk's office Portsmouth Town Book, 412, Nov. 15, 1662, he was "about 56." In *George Fox Digg'd Out of His Burrowes, Writings*, V, lxiv, he writes he was "now about three-score years." He is "aged about seventie-five years" in Testimony given Feb. 7, 1677/78, *Publication Rhode Island Historical Society*, 1900, VIII, 157. On July 2, 1679, he is "now neare Four score years," *Rhode Island Colonial Records*, III 57.

6. Some guild members eventually became warders or even Master of the Company. That James Williams did not achieve these posi-

tions is seen by referring to C. M. Clode, *Early History of the Guild of Merchant Taylors* (London, 1888), I, 165; II, appendix I, 336ff. The record shows he did engage in land transactions with his brother-in-law James Pemberton, *Herts Genealogist and Antiquary*, ed. by William Brigg (Harpendon, 1899), III, 241–43.

7. G. Andrews Moriarty, *Rhode Island History* (1944) III, 23–30, 67–71, 91–102 gives data of the Pembertons in Saint Albans.

8. For the wills of James Williams and his wife Alice, consult Henry F. Waters, *New England Historical and Genealogical Register* (1889), XLIII, 291ff. Waters was the first to work out Williams' parentage and family relationships.

9. John Stow, *A Survey of London* (Oxford, 1908), II, 23–29.

10. For information on Williams' early education, I am indebted to Winslow's *Master Roger Williams*, 35–41.

11. C. M. Clode, *Memorials of the Guild of Merchant Taylors*, pp. 143–46.

12. *George Fox Digg'd, Writings*, V, ix.

13. Letter to John Winthrop, c. 1632, *Writings*, VI, 1–2.

14. John Strype, *Annals of the Reformation*, 4 vols. (Oxford, 1824), IV, 234–35.

15. Johannes Lindeboom, *Austin Friars: History of the Dutch Reformed Church in London 1550–1950* (The Hague, 1950).

16. William Ames (1576–1633) was one of an important group of ministers in Derbyshire, all of whom professed antiseparation while quietly accepting the doctrine of the Separatists. He was the author of two important works, *Medulla Theologiae* and *De Conscientia*, in which he spelled out significant features of Congregational polity: granting of membership only to the proved elect and the autonomy of particular congregations.

17. Champlin Burrage, *The Early English Dissenters*, 2 vols. (Cambridge, 1912), I, 144–48.

18. Various versions exist of how Coke and Williams may have met. Most probably it was in the Star Chamber, where the young boy may have been taking shorthand, only recently invented, involving Merchant Taylors and foreign workmen of their craft. See Clode, *Early History of the Guild of Merchant Taylors*, I, 75ff.

19. Written by Mrs. Sadleir on the outside of Williams' first letter to her during his trip to England in 1652. See *Writings*, VI, 252ff.

20. *Ibid.*, 239ff.

21. G. S. Davies, *Charterhouse in London* (London, 1929), p. 201.

22. In turning what had previously been a monastery and then a town house into a preparatory school for the university, Coke defeated the efforts of his inveterate enemy, Sir Francis Bacon, who wished to convert the establishment into a school for servants.

23. Quoted, James Bass Mullinger, *The University of Cambridge,* 3 vols. (Cambridge, 1884), II, 142.

24. David Masson, *The Life of John Milton,* 4 vols. (New York, 1946), I, 274–75.

25. See S. E. Morison, *The Founding of Harvard College* (Cambridge, 1935), p. 70.

26. *Ibid.,* p. 77.

27. John Milton, *Of Education,* 1644 edition.

28. *The Bloudy Tenent, Writings,* III, 305; *The Hireling Ministry None of Christs, Writings,* VII, 169.

29. *Ibid.,* III, 306.

30. Quoted, Winslow, *Roger Williams,* 65.

31. Quoted, Thomas Fuller, *The Church-History of Britain* (London, 1655), Bk. X, pp. 108–10.

32. Quoted, Mullinger, *The University of Cambridge,* III, 566–67.

33. Quoted in O. S. Straus, *Roger Williams: The Pioneer of Religious Liberty* (New York, 1894), pp. 8–9.

34. *Writings,* VI, 356.

35. *Diary of Lady Margaret Hoby,* 1599–1605, edited by Dorothy M. Meads (London, 1930), tells how her chaplain, a "Mr. Rhodes," was really kept busy seven days a week to keep up with her sense of religiosity.

36. *Collections Rhode Island Historical Society,* XXIX, 71.

37. Barrington Correspondence, British Museum, Egerton MSS2645. A film of the Barrington letters in this collection is now owned by Yale University.

38. Williams' two letters to Lady Barrington are printed in *New England Historical and Genealogical Register,* XLIII (1889), 315–20.

39. *Collections Rhode Island Historical Society,* XV, 64.

40. *The Bloody Tenent Yet More Bloody, Writings,* IV, 64.

41. *Ibid.,* VI, 239. Williams admits that "Bishop Laud pursued me out of this land."

42. Different versions of this idea were repeated at various times in Williams' life.

## Chapter Two

1. *Writings,* VI, 263.

2. Brockunier, *Roger Williams,* 281.

3. John Winthrop, *History of New England,* 2 vols. (Boston, 1853), I, 340. Hereafter cited as *Journal.*

4. Hubbard, the official historian of the Bay, even lied to make Williams look bad for posterity. Not at all mentioned by Winthrop, who knew all about the famous episode in which Endecott cut out

the cross in the English flag, Williams was still singled out by Hubbard as the instigator of the episode. See William Hubbard, *General History of New England, 2 Collections Massachusetts Historical Society*, V, 205–6. Morton made Williams out to be a troublemaker, who, unable to win many of the Plymouth congregation over to his unorthodox ideas, sought to be dismissed from his post there. See Nathaniel Morton, *New England's Memorial* (Boston, 1855), 102. Mather's description of Williams' having a windmill in his head was of course the most damaging indictment the orthodoxy leveled at their foe. See Mather, *Magnalia Christi Americana* (London, 1702), p. 9. Yet Mather realized Williams possessed much substance and referred to him as one whom "judicious people" felt "had the root of the matter in him."

5. Almost until the time of his death, Winthrop cared deeply for his younger friend. It was he who warned Williams to escape when the Bay magistrates meant to apprehend him in early 1636 in order to return him to England. See *Writings*, VI, 335. Bradford regarded Williams as "a man godly and zealous, having many precious parts," but later changed his account to have it accord with the disparaging views being set forth by the Bay. See Bradford, *The History Of Plimouth Plantation* (Boston, 1898), Bk. II, pp. 369–70.

6. *Journal*, I, 49–51.
7. Williams to John Cotton, Jr., 1671, *Writings*, VI, 356.
8. *Journal*, I, 63.
9. *The Bloody Tenent Yet More Bloody, Writings*, IV, 461.
10. *Journal*, I, 139.
11. *History Of Plimouth Plantation*, 369–70.
12. *Journal*, I, 145–46.
13. *Ibid.*, I, 145, 147.
14. *Ibid.*, I, 180.
15. *Massachusetts Bay Records*, I, 115.
16. *Journal*, I, 193–94.
17. *Ibid.*, I, 195.
18. *Ibid.*, I, 198.
19. *Massachusetts Bay Records*, I, 160–61; *Journal*, I, 204.
20. *Letter of John Cotton, Writings*, I, 324–25.
21. *The Bloudy Tenent, Writings*, III, 73.
22. *Journal*, I, 209-10.
23. See Williams' 1682 Testimony, *Writings*, VI, 407.
24. *Journal*, I, 209ff.
25. From Williams' 1677 Testimony, Rider's *Historical Tracts*, No. 14, 55.
26. *Rhode Island Colonial Records*, I, 14.
27. *Writings*, VI, 3–7.

28. Papers of William Harris, *Collections Rhode Island Historical Society* (1902), p. 203.

29. The Initial Deed is printed in Howard M. Chapin's *Documentary History of Rhode Island*, 2 vols. (Providence, 1916, 1919), I, 76–78.

30. *Writings*, VI, 6.

31. *Journal*, II, 342–44.

32. *Rhode Island Colonial Records*, I, 143–46.

33. *Ibid.*, p. 145.

34. *Writings*, VI, 262–66.

35. *Rhode Island Colonial Records*, I, 316–17.

36. Isaac Backus, *A History of New England, with Particular Reference to the Denomination of Christians called Baptists, 2 vols.* (Newton, Mass., 1871).

37. *Writings*, VI, 279.

38. *Rhode Island Colonial Records*, I, 327.

39. *Writings*, VI, 319.

40. *Ibid.*, p. 342.

41. *Collections, Rhode Island Historical Society*, IV, 111.

42. *Ibid.*, XV, 421; *Providence Records*, VIII, 122.

### Chapter Three

1. *George Fox Digg'd, Writings*, V, 412–13.

2. *A Key into the Language of America, Writings*, I, 1–219.

3. Winthrop's assertion that the natives possessed only "a natural right" to the land and that the colonists has as much right to it as the Indians so long as they left them "sufficient for their use," ultimately allowed the Bay to take as much land as they desired. See "Reasons for the Plantation" printed in R. C. Winthrop, *Life and Letters of John Winthrop*, I, 309–10.

4. *New England's Prospect* (Boston, 1865), p. 103.

5. From his 1677 Testimony, Rider's *Historical Tracts*, No. 14, p. 53.

6. *Key, Writings*, I, 19.

7. *Ibid.*, p. 27.

8. Robert Baillie, *Dissuasive from the Errours of the Time* (London, 1645), p. 60.

9. Thomas Lechford, *Plain Dealing, 3 Collections Massachusetts Historical Society*, III, 80, 109.

10. *Key, Writings*, I, 25.

11. *Rhode Island Colonial Records*, II, 162.

12. Chapin, *Documentary History*, I, 212–13.

13. *Apologeticall Narration*, 24. See William Haller's *Tracts on Liberty in the Puritan Revolution*, 3 vols., New York, 1933.

14. Robert Baillie, *Letters and Journals of Robert Baillie*, ed. David Laing (London, 1841–42), 2 vols., July 23, 1644, II, 211, 212.

15. *Writings*, I, 314–96.

16. *Ibid.*, p. 315.

17. *Ibid.*, p. 319.

18. *Ibid.*, p. 320.

19. *The Bloody Tenent Yet More Bloody, Writings*, IV, 29.

20. *The Bloudy Tenent, Writings*, III, 206.

21. *Mr. Cotton's Letter Examined and Answered, Writings*, I, 323–324.

22. *Queries, Writings*, II, 254–75.

23. William Haller, *Liberty and Reformation in the Puritan Revolution* (New York, 1955), p. 150.

24. *Queries, Writings*, II, 255.

25. *The Bloudy Tenent, Writings*, III, 3–4.

26. *Massachusetts Bay Records*, I, 142.

27. *The Bloudy Tenent*, pp. 250, 356.

28. *Commons Journals*, August 9, 1644.

29. William Prynne, *Twelve Considerable Serious Questions touching Church Government* (London, 1644), p. 7.

30. James Ernest, "Roger Williams and the English Revolution," *Rhode Island Historical Society Collections*, XXIV, 1–28, 118–28.

31. Haller, *Liberty and Reformation in the Puritan Revolution*, p. 278.

32. *Christenings, Writings*, VII, 31–41. Assumed lost, this publication was found in 1881 by Henry Martyn Dexter in the Thomasin Collection of Commonwealth Pamphlets in the British Museum.

33. *The Bloudy Tenent*, III, 400.

34. *Christenings*, p. 32.

## Chapter Four

1. It was fundamentally a policy of divide and conquer that the Bay pursued in their treatment of the Indians. In alienating tributary tribes like the Mohegans from their overlords, the Narragansetts, the Bay leaders thus thwarted the building of large Indian forces who could threaten them as they systematically went about their business of robbing the Indians of their land.

2. *Massachusetts Bay Records*, III, 49.

3. *Ibid.*, pp. 196–97, 201–2.

4. *Journal*, II, 342–44.

5. Williams to Endecott, *Writings*, IV, 504.

6. *Rhode Island Colonial Records*, I, Sept. 1, 1651, 234–35.

7. S. R. Gardiner, *History of the Commonwealth and Protectorate* (New York, 1897–1903), II, 207–10.

8. *Writings*, VI, 236.

9. H. E. Turner, "William Coddington," *Rhode Island Historical Tracts*, IV, 41, 47–49.

10. *Writings*, VI, 236.

11. *Ibid.*, p. 260.

12. *Ibid.*, p. 262.

13. *Providence Records*, XV, 63.

14. Letter of July 12, 1654, *Writings*, VI, 261–62.

15. Williams to Mrs. Sadleir, *Ibid.*, p. 238.

16. *Ibid.*, p. 241.

17. *Ibid.*, p. 244.

18. *Ibid.*, pp. 246, 249–53.

19. Gardiner, *History of the Commonwealth and Protectorate*, II, 28.

20. Masson, *Milton*, IV, 391–92.

21. *The Fourth Paper Presented by Major Butler*, *Writings*, VII, 119–141.

22. *The Hireling Ministry None of Christs*, *Writings*, VII, 147–91. The term *hireling* referring to ministers who were paid by the state for their work had been previously used by George Fox, the Quaker leader. The next six parenthetical references in the text refer to the page numbers in *The Hireling Ministry None of Christs*.

23. Hubbard *History*, 2 *Collections Massachusetts Historical Society*, VI, 338.

24. *John Cotton's Answer to Roger Williams*, *Writings*, II, 136–37.

25. *The Bloody Tenent Yet More Bloody*, *Writings*, IV, 64.

26. *Cotton's Answer*, p. 137.

27. *The Hireling Ministry*, pp. 162–63.

28. *Journal*, II, 30.

29. *The Hireling Ministry*, p. 158.

30. *Ibid.*, p. 168.

31. *Ibid.*, p. 176.

32. *The Bloody Tenent Yet More Bloody*, *Writings*, IV.

33. *Letter to John Cotton, Jr.*, VI, 353.

34. Backus, *The Baptists*, I, 246.

35. *The Bloody Tenent Yet More Bloody*, p. 81.

36. *Letter to John Cotton, Jr.*, VI, 353.

37. *Experiments of Spiritual Life and Health*, *Writings*, VII, 45–115.

38. *The Examiner Defended*, *Writings*, VII, 195–279. James Ernst first identified the tract while rummaging through the Thomasin Collection of Commonwealth Pamphlets in preparation for his book on Williams.

*Chapter Five*

1. *Writings*, V.
2. *Ibid.*, p. 59.
3. *Ibid.*, p. 305.
4. *Rhode Island Colonial Records*, I, 375–78.
5. Williams to United Colonies, 2 *Proceedings Massachusetts Historical Society*, III, 258–59. Williams accused Harris of caring no more for the Quakers than for the Baptists, his prior affiliation.
6. *George Fox Digg'd*, p. 3.
7. "To the People Called Quakers," unpaged.
8. *Ibid.*, pp. 102–3.

# Selected Bibliography

## Bibliography

A bibliography of Roger Williams is sorely needed. The entries in the third volume of the *Literary History of the United States* (1957) and its *Bibliographic Supplement* (1959) can only serve as a start in this direction.

The main outline of Williams' life can be obtained from his writings, but for an appreciation of his public life and career *The Early Records of The Town of Providence*, 21 vols., 1892–1915, and the *Records of the Colony of Rhode Island and Providence Plantations*, 10 vols. (Providence, 1856–65), must be consulted. The writings of such New England contemporaries like Winthrop, John Clarke, Edward Winslow, Samuel Gorton, William Bradford, and others help us to see Williams from various points of view. For any thoughtful consideration of Williams' thinking in relation to his time, the pamphlet literature of the 1640's must be studied, a good introduction to which is provided in William Haller's *Tracts on Liberty in the Puritan Revolution*, 3 vols. (New York, 1933–34).

For an understanding of the Puritan mind and its workings in early America the works of Perry Miller are indispensable. These include *The New England Mind: The Seventeenth Century* (New York, 1939); *The New England Mind: From Colony to Province* (Cambridge, 1954); and *Orthodoxy in Massachusetts* (Cambridge, 1933).

### PRIMARY SOURCES

Collected Editions

*The Writings of Roger Williams.* 6 vols. Providence: *Narragansett Club Publications*, 1866–74. This was the first collection of the separate works and most of the letters.

*The Complete Writings of Roger Williams.* 7 vols. New York: Russell and Russell, 1963. A reprint of the *Narragansett Club Publications;* this set has added a seventh volume containing several short pamphlets hitherto not easily accessible.

Separate Works (Arranged in order of publication)

A *Key into the Language of America*. London: n.p., 1643, *Writings*, I.

*Mr. Cotton's Letter Lately Printed, Examined and Answered*. 1644. *Writings*, I.

*Queries of Highest Consideration*. London: n.p., 1644, *Writings*, II.

*The Bloudy Tenent of Persecution, for cause of Conscience, discussed in A.*

*Conference betweene Truth and Peace*. London: n.p., 1644, *Writings*, III.

*Christenings Make Not Christians*. London: n.p., 1645, *Writings*, VII.

*Experiments of Spiritual Life and Health*, written c. 1650, London: n.p., 1652, *Writings*, VII.

*The Fourth Paper Presented by Major Butler*. London: n.p., 1652, *Writings*, VII.

*The Bloody Tenent Yet More Bloody*, written c. 1648–50, London: n.p., 1652, *Writings*, IV.

*The Hireling Ministry None of Christs*. London: n.p., 1652, *Writings*, VII.

*The Examiner Defended*. London: n.p., 1652, *Writings*, VII.

*George Fox Digg'd Out of His Burrowes*. Boston: n.p., 1676, *Writings*, V.

*Letters of Roger Williams*. 1632–82, *Writings*, VI.

Edited Texts and Reprints

A *Key into the Language of America*, reprinted in part in *Collections Massachusetts Historical Society*, III (1794), 203–38 and V (1798), 80–106; a reprint of the complete text can be found in *Collections Rhode Island Historical Society*, I (1827), 17–163.

A reprint of *Christenings Make Not Christians*, edited by Henry M. Dexter, is to be found in *Rhode Island Historical Tracts*, 1st ser., No. 14, 1881.

*Experiments of Spiritual Life and Health*. Introduction by Winthrop S. Hudson, Philadelphia, 1951.

*The Fourth Paper Presented by Major Butler*. Edited by Clarence S. Brigham, has been reprinted by the Club for Colonial Reprints of Providence, Rhode Island.

### SECONDARY SOURCES

1. Biography and Criticism (most significant full-length biographies and studies in order of publication)

KNOWLES, JAMES D. *Memoirs of Roger Williams*. Boston: Lincoln Edmons and Company, 1834. A sprightly yet thoughtful and scholarly work by a Baptist professor. Contains many letters and documents not to be found elsewhere.

ELTON, ROMEO. *Life of Roger Williams.* Providence: A. Cockshaw, 1853. Contains the essential facts and is sympathetic in its approach.

BACKUS, ISAAC. *A History of New England, with Particular Reference to the Denomination of Christians called Baptists.* 2 vols. Newton, Mass.: The Backus Historical Society, 1871. Makes the point that Williams' great contribution to American life was his insistence on both religious and civil liberty.

TYLER, MOSES COIT. *A History of American Literature, 1706–1765.* 2 vols. New York: George H. Putnam, 1878; reprinted in 1962. In having founded a colony where church and state were separate, Williams fixed "for all time, the barriers against tyranny on the one side, and lawlessness on the other."

STRAUS, OSCAR S. *The Pioneer of Religious Liberty.* New York: Century Company, 1894. Williams' contribution to American civilization is seen in the title Straus selected for his book.

CARPENTER, EDMUND J. *Roger Williams: A Study of the Life, Times and Character of a Political Pioneer.* New York: Grafton Press, 1909. A well-written, judicious account. Sees Williams primarily as a controversialist. Important for background material on English Separatism.

PARRINGTON, VERNON L. *Main Currents in American Thought.* New York: Harcourt, Brace and Company, 1927–30. Seen as an early exponent of Jeffersonian liberalism, Williams is equated as a political philosopher rather than as a theologian.

EASTON, EMILY. *Roger Williams: Prophet and Pioneer.* Boston: Houghton Mifflin Company, 1930. Very readable and important for its stress on Williams' early life in England.

ERNST, JAMES E. *Roger Williams: New England Firebrand.* New York: The MacMillan Company, 1932. A valuable book seriously marred by lack of careful documentation. The emphasis is on Williams as primarily a political thinker.

BROCKUNIER, SAMUEL HUGH. *The Irrepressible Democrat: Roger Williams.* New York: Ronald Press Company, 1940. Probably the best biography so far written but weakened by undue emphasis on Williams as a democrat.

DOS PASSOS, JOHN. *The Ground We Stand On.* New York: Harcourt, Brace and Company, 1941. Written in the exciting Dos Passos manner, the work suffers from the undue significance given Williams' ideas, which are regarded as "bringing the seeds of a whole civilization" to a new land.

ROSSITER, CLINTON. *Seedtime of the Republic*. New York: Harcourt, Brace and Company, 1953. Williams presented as having demonstrated that an enduring civil society could hold forth in Rhode Island without the help of a national church.

WINSLOW, OLA ELIZABETH. *Master Roger Williams*. New York: The MacMillan Company, 1957. An excellent and sympathetic work, with the England of the Stuarts in which Williams grew up skillfully presented. Underemphasizes her protagonist's religious thought in moulding his life and ideals.

MILLER, PERRY. *Roger Williams*. New York: The Bobbs-Merrill Company, 1953. A brief judicious account of Williams' life and ideas together with representative selections from his writings.

COVEY, CYCLONE. *The Gentle Radical: Roger Williams*. New York: The Macmillan Company, 1966. The most detailed account yet of Williams' first nine years in New England. The interrelationship of Williams and the New Englanders who figure in his life is excellently done.

## 2. Special Studies in Books and Periodicals (arranged in order of publication)

DEXTER, HENRY M. *As to Roger Williams, and His "Banishment" from the Massachusetts Plantation*. Boston: Congregational Publishing Society, 1876. A last-ditch defense of the Bay's banishment of Williams in view of the latter's "seditious, defiant, and pernicious posture toward the State."

BURRAGE, HENRY S. "Why Was Roger Williams Banished?" *American Journal of Theology*, V (1901), 1–17. A refutation of Dexter's position in which it is made absolutely clear that Williams was sent into exile solely for religious and not political ideas.

ERNST, JAMES E. *The Political Thought of Roger Williams*. Seattle: Washington University, 1929. An overly systematized and repetitious book making Williams out to be a political democrat.

————. "New Light on Roger Williams' Life in England," *Collection Rhode Island Historical Society*, XXII (1929), 97–103. Several letters, hitherto unpublished, help fill out Williams' life as a chaplain at Otes.

————. "Roger Williams and the English Revolution," *ibid.*, XXIV (1931), 1–58, 118–28. The influence Williams' writings may have had on the various sects, especially the Levellers, in seeking a greater sense of political democracy.

PARKES, HENRY B. "John Cotton and Roger Williams Debate Toleration, 1644–1652," *New England Quarterly*, IV (1931), 735–56.

Cotton is viewed as having emerged from the Middle Ages; Williams, as an exponent of twentieth-century thinking.

FREUND, MICHAEL. "Roger Williams, Apostle of Complete Religious Liberty," *Collection Rhode Island Historical Society*, XXVI (1933), 101–33. This article is a translation by James E. Ernst of a chapter in Freund's *Der Idee Der Toleranz im England der Grossen Revolution* (Halle: M. Niemeyer, 1927). Williams' basic position is seen as hinging on the premise that because the civil state derived from the natural order, it could not possibly concern itself with religion, which belonged to the spiritual kingdom.

STEAD, GEORGE A. "Roger Williams and the Massachusetts-Bay," *New England Quarterly*, VII (1934), 235–57. Williams' banishment was necessary in light of his undermining the authority of the Bay court "by his telling appeals to the Puritan civil conscience."

WIENER, FREDERICK B. "Roger Williams' Contribution to Modern Thought," *Collection Rhode Island Historical Society*, XXVIII (1935), 1–20. Williams' contribution lay in presenting the idea that the state existed for the people and not the other way around.

HARKNESS, REUBEN, E. E. "Roger Williams: Prophet of Tomorrow," *Journal of Religion*, XV (1935), 400–25. A prophet in the sense of his love for people whom he wished to be the recipients of his ideas.

ANDREWS, CHARLES M. "Roger Williams and the Founding of Rhode Island," *The Colonial Period of American History*, II (1936), 1–36. Fact-filled yet extremely readable essay.

HIRSCH, ELIZABETH. "John Cotton and Roger Williams: Their Controversy Concerning Religious Liberty," *Church History*, X (1941), 38–51. An attempt to make Cotton appear as a deeper and more practical man than Williams.

SWAN, B. F. "Roger Williams and the Insane," *Rhode Island History*, V (1946), 65–70. From a few letters he wrote on the subject, it was evident that Williams thought it was the civil government's duty to care for the insane.

ROSSITER, CLINTON. "Roger Williams on the Anvil of Experience," *American Quarterly*, III (1951), 14–21. Founding Rhode Island and seeing to its continued welfare caused Williams to learn much from practical experience which his theoretical political principles had not prepared him for.

CALAMANDREI, MAURO. "Neglected Aspects of Roger Williams' Thought," *Church History*, XXI (1952), 239–58. Shows Williams' theology to have been a far more important influence on his thought than had hitherto been believed.

SIMPSON, ALAN. "How Democratic Was Roger Williams?" *William and Mary Quarterly*, XIII (1956), 53–67. Presents Williams as far more interested in religious liberty than with the operation of the civil state; even when engaged in the latter activity, he was not the democrat in the sense that the English Levellers were.

## 3. Background

A study of Williams' life and thought is to take in literally almost every important phase of seventeenth-century thought. Besides the books mentioned in the text, for the number of works one can consult, the reader is referred to the bibliographies in Calamandrei's and Roddy's theses as well as to the more voluminous ones in Arthur E. Barker's *Milton and the Puritan Dilemma* (Toronto: University of Toronto Press, 1942), and Perry Miller's *The New England Mind*. Roger Williams and the Massachusetts Magistrates, edited by Theodore P. Greene (Boston: D. C. Heath and Company, 1964), has a good bibliography on the whole question of religious liberty.

# Index

74371